NATURAL	REPENT		BORN
BORN IN SIN	*The Mystery of God Revealed*		OF GOD
DEATH			LIFE

A World Deceived

(Rev 12:9)

... true wisdom that will shock the world

Andy G. van den Berg

FSMI Publishing
Halifax, Nova Scotia

Copyright © 2005 FSMI Publishing

Published by FSMI Publishing.
Web site: www.aworlddeceived.ca
Email: fsmi@ns.sympatico.ca

Project Editor: Bronwen Hook
Web site design: Bev Lamb
Cover design: Dianne and Andy van den Berg

Printed and bound in Canada.

Library and Archives Canada Cataloguing in Publication

van den Berg, Andy G., 1946-

    A world deceived (Rev 12:9) : ...true wisdom that will shock the world / Andy van den Berg.

Includes bibliographical references and index.
ISBN 0-9737016-0-9

1. Christianity—Essence, genius, nature. 2. Repentance.

3. Deception.   I. Title.

BT60.V35 2005   230   C2004-906972-1

Contents

Acknowledgements 4

Introduction 5

The Beginning 11

Of the World 23

Conversion 25

Repent 29

Born of God 33

The Mystery Babylon 41

Popes and the Princes of this World 53

Shroud of Turin a Hoax 61

Christmas: Strictly a Pagan Celebration 65

Easter: Strictly a Pagan Celebration 71

Foundations Out of Course 77

The Mystery of God Revealed 81

Fellow Servants 91

The Virgin Birth and the Appearances of Mary .. 95

Sainthood by the Pope 101

The Abomination of Desolation 107

Spiritual Blindness 111

Soldiers for Christ 129

The Future 153

Notes and References 160

Acknowledgements

We thank our Heavenly Father and our Lord and Savior Jesus Christ for having revealed to us all things and for giving us the courage and strength to go forth with the message of truth and the writing of this book. Many thanks also to my dear wife Dianne and our children, Chris and Angela, and their families for their support. We thank God for revealing Himself to our dear friends and their family. As fellow soldiers for Christ we are grateful for their steadfastness in the faith and for their prayers during times of need.

We also wish to thank all those that have contributed to the completion and publication of this book.

To Maggie,

Seek and ye shall find.
(Matt. 7:7)

Rudy van den Berg

July 15/17

4

NATURAL	REPENT	SPIRITUAL
BORN IN SIN		BORN OF GOD
DEATH		LIFE

Introduction

As my wife and I came into our faith in the mid-eighties, we were eager to start sharing our new-found wisdom. Little did we know then the consequences of sharing the truth concerning the true and living God and the spirit we were dealing with. This we only started to experience when we reached out to people and learned how they reacted to our message. When people requested information by phone or by letter and asked that we share our message with them, we sent them copies of articles I had written, accompanied with a letter of introduction. Some of the articles became part of this book so we thought it was only fitting to start this book with the same message.

Our Letter

Blessed be God, the Father of our Lord Jesus Christ, who has blessed us with all wisdom and knowledge and who has made known to us the mysteries of his Gospel as was proclaimed by the Lord Jesus Christ and the brethren who have gone before us.

We thank Him for revealing Himself to us through the Lord Jesus Christ and for allowing us to share this mystery with you.

As you read and, we hope, study parts of our testimony, which is after Christ, you will note that our faith stands not in the wisdom of men but in the power of

God (1 Cor 2:4-8). The Gospel we preach is not after man but by the revelation of our Lord and Savior Jesus Christ (Gal 1:11,12).

Most people claim the things we speak of to be of mere foolishness (1 Cor 2:14), while some others even will classify us as evildoers (1 Peter 3:16). To those that believe, however, there will be no condemnation, as it will be to them a word of truth and the Gospel of their salvation.

Since the days of our teaching (John 6:45) and the high calling which has been granted to us, we are fully aware of how our testimony of Christ pulls down every stronghold of this world (religions, medical profession, etc.). We know how it casts down every imagination and every high thing that exalts itself against the knowledge of God (2 Cor 10:4,5) and how it shakes the very foundation of this world.

Approximately 2000 years ago, the Jews truly thought that they knew Abraham and Moses and that they served the true and living God. However, when God dwelt amongst them, they crucified Him, as the Gospel He preached convinced them that their deeds were evil (John 3:19). The Gentiles today truly believe that they know Christ and that they follow after His ways, while they have been deceived in like manner (Rev 12:9).

Since the formation of the Roman Church, literally a myriad of other religions have sprung up, whose foundation is not after Christ, but after the workings of the spirit of mankind (darkness) and has absolutely nothing to do with the true foundation brought forth by Christ.

Even twentieth century Pentecostalism has, since the early days of the Azusa Street Revival in 1906, been divided into hundreds of different groups, as a result of the division from within (spirit of darkness).

Since God opened our eyes and gave us a true vision, it is very clear by the fruits of religion, that they serve a false Christ, a man-made image of a false God, in which there is no salvation.

Even historical facts clearly show that celebrations such as Christmas, Good Friday and Easter are pagan celebrations and have nothing to do with the birth, death and resurrection of Christ.

I liken religion to a copier machine. Every manufacturer (denomination) has its own version of God, but none of the copies they produce is the original "One". Yes, Satan is a master deceiver (Rev 12:9) and has most of mankind convinced that he is a God. He is even using the word of God, but not in truth. He is also trying to duplicate God's gifts, but again not in truth.

At what level has this world been deceived then? Let us go back to the words spoken by the Lord Jesus Christ two thousand years ago, which teach us about the deception that is in this world today.

Matt 24:24. For there shall arise false Christs and false prophets, and shall show great signs and wonders; insomuch that, if it were possible, they shall deceive the very elect.

Mankind still remains separated from God and travels a way not knowing where he is going. He reads the Bible but is not able to understand one word, as it is just a story to him, with no spiritual meaning (1 Cor 2:14). For this reason man does not understand any of the words or the parables and has his own interpretation thereof.

Back in 1985-1987, I testified to many and warned them how God would visit their sin. They included

Jimmy Swaggart, Ralph Rutledge, Jimmy and Tammy Bakker and the hierarchy of the Catholic church. God did manifest Himself and clearly showed them that they were not the servants of the true and living God but instead revealed who their real father was (John 8:44). But even after their fall and scandals, involving arch-bishops, bishops, priests and ministers of all denominations, even then, they still did not want to believe that God had sent me with a message of truth. Scripture is always true when it says: "Men loved darkness rather than light" (John 3:19).

Let it be known that, in the coming years, the religions of this world will be severely tested as God will bring them to an open shame and clearly show them what spirit they serve. As a result of this threat to their security they will all unite into one religion (evangelization), only to find out for themselves how they have been deceived through the divisions within.

The question remains now: how can you know the difference, and how can you know that my doctrine is not of my own but of the One that sent me?

In order to know my Father in Heaven, the true and living God, you must first turn to Him (see Chapter 5 on "Repentance").

Only then will He teach you in all things (John 6:45) and only then will He be able to reveal Himself to you and will you be able to do His will. Only then will you know that the doctrine I speak of is of God, and not of myself (John 7:16,17).

You need not that any man teach you (1 John 2:27); God will teach you in all things. However, presently you are going the wrong way and will never know God as you follow after a false God (darkness). It is like a tow-truck – in order to be pulled in the right direction, both vehicles need to be facing the same way.

Therefore, you must first turn around (acknowledging that you are a sinner and separated from God) in order for God to be able to draw you towards Him (John 6:44).

I know that we will never hear from most of you as you take pride in following after a false God or a false Christ, rather than seeking Him in truth (Ps 145:18).

The road to salvation is a very narrow one and few there be that find it (John 7:14).

However, to those that desire to seek God in truth, we encourage you to read this book with an open mind. It will show you, step by step, how deception has entered into this world, it will teach you the process of repentance and how one must turn from the power of Satan unto God in order to become a child of God. We hope that by reading this book you will be convinced to start searching for the true and living God. You don't have to knock hard in order for the door to the truth to be opened. Just ask and you will receive, as we did. It is our hope that reading this book will help you in your search for that narrow road that leads to the Kingdom of God. It is only our Father in Heaven who can give you the key of knowledge to know the difference between good and evil.

Do not be disturbed by the things you read and, above all, we hope that you will not be offended.

Matt 11:16: BLESSED IS HE, WHOSOEVER SHALL NOT BE OFFENDED IN ME.

In the love and service of our Lord and Savior Jesus Christ.

Matt 13:37-39

He that soweth the good seed is the Son of man; the field is the world; the good seed are the children of the kingdom; but the tares are the children of the wicked one; the enemy that sowed them is the devil; the harvest is the end of the world; and the reapers are the angels.

NATURAL	REPENT		SPIRITUAL
BORN IN SIN			BORN OF GOD
DEATH			LIFE

The Beginning

I was born on November 24, 1946, in the small town of Hoogkarspel in the province of North-Holland, located in the North West of Holland. I was the sixth child in what eventually became a family of nine children. There were five boys and four girls and I was the youngest boy. My parents named me Adrie but, as they were devoted catholics, at the ritual of baptism I was given a whole series of other names: Adrianus Gerardus Johannes. As I went through the ritual of what was called "confirmation" at the age of twelve, they added the name of Willibrordus, a so-called Dutch saint.

During the early years of my life, my mother had a very difficult time trying to feed me. I was unable to keep any food down and as a result I did not gain any weight. I believe I had a problem with my pyloric valve, which seemed to correct itself as I grew up. Nevertheless, there was many times my mother and father thought that I would not survive. At an early age (I think it was at the age of six) they even sent me to a sanitorium for six weeks during the summer, in the hope that I would gain some weight.

When I was ten years old my family moved to the Noord Oost Polder. The Dutch are well recognized for building dikes and claiming new land from the sea, and the Noord Oost Polder was an area that was part of the Zuiderzee and had become the new land where many farmers settled after the Second World War.

As I grew up, I was a very active child with above-average scholastic abilities. My main activity was soccer and I played on the first team of the local soccer association at the age of 16. Considering that most people playing on the team ranged in age from 20 to 30, this was quite an accomplishment. I enjoyed the home games in particular, as many of my family members, including my father, would often attend. I was a skinny boy, but despite my physical limitations, I played center forward and that same year we won the divisional championship during an away game and were promoted to the next division. This created a lot of excitement in the local community: we were all placed on the local fire truck and, with the local band in front, we were paraded through the town.

I was raised to believe that the youngest boy of a family should join the priesthood and, as I grew up, I was constantly reminded that I would attend the seminary. Even so, I was devastated and terribly homesick when my parents drove me to the seminary, when I was 12 years old, where over 700 other young man between the ages of 12 and 20 studied for the priesthood. We were only allowed home visits during Christmas, Easter and the summer holidays and I was always sad to have to leave my home and family to return to the seminary. (It is interesting to note that during a recent visit to Holland, some 44 years later, the seminary is no longer in existence and has been turned into a police academy.)

Seminary was not my strong point: studying six languages (including Latin and Greek), algebra and science became a horrible burden and I could not wait for the weekend when a soccer game would often be scheduled.

I was terribly homesick and studying soon gave way to mischievous acts that, late during my second year,

I was born in Holland in 1946 and was the youngest boy in a family of nine children.

I (bottom left) entered the seminary at the age of 12, where over 700 other young men between the ages of 12 and 20 studied for the priesthood.

During a recent visit to Holland, I learned that the seminary is no longer in existence and has been turned into a police academy. The main church and chapels had been changed into a conference hall.

resulted in my departure from the seminary. After leaving the seminary, I continued my education for a few more years before specializing in horticulture.

During the summer we all worked very hard on the family farm. Most mornings we rose at six and harvesting tulip bulbs kept us busy throughout the summer. Since my dad grew all sorts of crops there was always a lot of work and often there was little time for recreation.

Despite the hard work, I have very good memories of my childhood, and the work ethic that was instilled in me has benefited me throughout my life. I was always very active and, besides soccer, there were many other things that interested me. The town I grew up in had a small amphitheater and, once a year, I participated in a small theater group that put on a play. My mother was very much involved with a local choir, and she convinced me they needed some younger members. So I found myself not only straining my vocal cords in the general choir, but also in the church choir. Besides the regular soccer practices, choirs, acting, and fishing whenever I could find some time, I also joined a youth organization that organized weekend dances, sporting activities and other events. It was not long before I became the local secretary, and just about every evening was occupied with some kind of an activity.

It was during this time that I received information about an exchange program to Canada for young men with an agricultural/horticultural background. It was not easy to gain parental approval but I was eventually allowed to join a group of 90 young men in the summer of 1967 for a three-month stay in Canada. I was very excited, as this was not only my first trip abroad but also my first flying experience. We left Schiphol airport in Amsterdam and we flew for 14 hours non-stop on a DC-7 propeller-powered aircraft to Toronto. After a bus ride to downtown Toronto, we all gathered at Union Station (the central train station) and there I learned that I would be one of a group of six to travel to Digby, Nova Scotia, and work on a provincially owned farm called Beaver Brook Farms. The main objective of the project was to create employment for the local people and the main crops were strawberries and blueberries.

This was the year of Expo in Montreal and on the train ride to Saint John, New Brunswick, we decided to spend a few days in Montreal and visit Expo. Living on hot dogs and hamburgers for a few days, it was not long before we all ran out of money. When we arrived in Saint John, we found our way to the ferry terminal to take the ride across the Bay of Fundy to Digby. A truck from Beaver Brook Farms soon picked us up and brought us to the small log cabin that would be our home. The following morning we learned that our responsibility would be to supervise the pickers, who were bussed in daily from the Digby area. It was a beautiful summer and each day we walked the strawberry fields after the morning fog had burned off and the strawberries were ready to be picked. Since we walked around most days in just shorts and sneakers we soon started to look like beach boys.

After our first month in Digby we became known as the six Dutch boys and on the weekends and the days that we were not able to work, we spent time walking the main street. Digby is a quaint little fishing town with a well-known scallop fleet. From where we were staying the walk into town via the old railroad tracks was quite a distance.

When we learned of a small apartment in town overlooking the Annapolis Basin, we soon packed our bags and moved.

One day we were hanging around the local war memorial, unable to work because of the rain, and I noticed an attractive young lady walking on the opposite side of the street.

I had no idea then that she would become my wife the following year.

Not long after this, I attended evening Mass at the Catholic church and—lo and behold—this same young woman sat right in front of me. After Mass, I was right behind her when she left and discovered that she lived just a few doors down from the church. When she entered her house, however, her father sent her back out to close his car windows and this brought us face to face. After I introduced myself, I invited her in the little English that I spoke, for a coke. Before leaving for the local restaurant, Dianne very politely introduced me to her parents. I learned at a later date that Dianne's father had turned around to her mother, after we had left and asked: "Who the hell was that?"

Dianne and me (and Pedro) in front of her family home in Digby, Nova Scotia, during the summer of 1967, when we met.

It was on that first evening that I learned that Dianne had been previously married for just two and a half years. Her husband Terry was killed in Montreal in a tragic car accident, coming home from work one night. When I met Dianne she had just returned home, nine months after the accident, to make a new beginning. After that first meeting Dianne and I saw each other on a regular basis.

Previously, one of the other Dutch boys and I had contacted the Department of Agriculture in Ontario seeking permanent employment. We were very shortly thereafter offered jobs at the Horticultural Institute in Vineland Station, a small community near St. Catherines. So, four weeks after I had met Dianne, we said goodbye at the Yarmouth airport, not knowing if we would ever see each other again.

It was not long before we received a telephone call explaining to us that, if we wanted to stay as a landed immigrant and continue our employment on a permanent basis, it was required that we go back to Holland and apply for immigration status there. Our employment status was guaranteed for a period of six weeks, as long as we returned within that time frame.

After having notified my parents that I would not be returning home as I had found permanent employment in Ontario, I had to send them a telegram that we would be returning with the rest of the exchange students as scheduled.

Since we only had six weeks to return to Vineland Station, I took the train to the Canadian Embassy in Den Haag at the first opportunity. After I had completed all of the necessary documentation, I learned that there was a one-year waiting list for new immigrants. However, confirmation of my employment with the Government of Ontario resulted in the issuance of my immigration visa within a few hours and soon I was back on the train home, knowing I would be leaving my family in Holland in the near future.

After our farewell at Yarmouth airport, Dianne and I continued to correspond and my family in Holland soon learned that I had met a Canadian girl, as there was a constant two-way flow of letters and cards.

Four weeks after I had come home, I was back at the airport in Amsterdam saying goodbye to my family, and what a sad affair it was, as none of us knew when we would see each other again.

In the meantime, Dianne had moved to Toronto to live with her brother and sister-in-law. She put Terry's death behind her and went back to work, finding employment as a secretary for a small company. It was good to see her again but, after spending one night in Toronto, I had to take the bus to Vineland Station to continue my employment as an agricultural technician. The job was most boring and I could not wait for Friday afternoons when I

At the Airport Schiphol in Amsterdam, Holland, just before immigrating to Canada.

took the bus to Toronto to spend the weekend with Dianne. Since her brother only had a small apartment, I usually stayed at the YMCA or a cheap hotel. Most of the time we tried to find things to do in the City, such as going to malls or for walks.

Within a few months, Dianne and I were engaged and were married on June 8, 1968. With Dianne's parents and brothers (she had another brother Wayne) and a few friends in attendance, we started our journey together. Life in the beginning was a real struggle. When we had decided to get married, I had left my job in

Vineland Station and, with my limited experience, finding a job in the big city of Toronto was not an easy task.

My first job in Toronto, on an order desk for a meat supply company, only lasted four weeks. With my limited skills in the English language, I must have mixed up too many orders and a week before we were to be married I was on the street looking for another job. As of the first Monday after we were married, I traveled almost two hours every morning and evening by bus to Richmond Hill (north of Toronto) where I had found a job delivering flowers for a greenhouse company.

The biggest struggle was the undiagnosed medical condition that I was born with, and the cold Canadian winter and changes in temperature became an almost unbearable burden.

The condition I suffered can best be described as a chronic sinus condition that affected the whole left side of my body. There were other brothers and sisters of my family in Holland that suffered from the same affliction. I was sent from one specialist to another and after numerous x-rays and a milogram test, they finally decided to make a correction through nose surgery. This, however, only worsened the situation and after trying every remedy available on the market, in the end I learned to live with it, although with great difficulty.

During this time we learned that Dianne was expecting our first child and on September 21, 1969, Christopher Andrew was born. My parents, who had been visiting us from Holland, just missed the birth of Christopher by one week.

Life became fairly routine for us after the birth of Christopher. Financially, things were difficult to manage. During her pregnancy Dianne experienced such terrible morning sickness (it lasted most of the day), that she left her job early on in her pregnancy.

At that time she was earning $150 per week and this left us only with only my weekly $80 paycheck to make ends meet.

The first years of our marriage, Dianne was kept busy raising Christopher while I supported the family by working six days a week for the greenhouse business. After a few years I decided to move on and became manager for a leading nursery business in Ontario.

In 1973 we became the proud owners of our first home in Alliston, Ontario, a small community a one-hour drive north of Toronto. The following year our daughter Angela Marie was born. Chris was just over four years old at the time and we were delighted with the fact that we now had a boy and a girl in the family.

Mark 10:6-9

But from the beginning of creation God made them male and female. For this cause shall a man leave his father and mother, and cleave to his wife; and they twain shall be one flesh: so then they are no more twain, but one flesh. What therefore God hath joined together, let no man put asunder.

NATURAL	REPENT	SPIRITUAL
BORN **IN** **SIN**		**BORN** **OF** **GOD**
DEATH		LIFE

Of the World

In 1973 I decided to change careers and started as a sales representative in the sales and marketing of industrial equipment. Being successful in sales was natural to me. I enjoyed it and through hard work (instilled in me as a young boy) and determination, I was well recognized by my peers for my success. Within 7 years I had gone from Sales Representative to Vice-President of Sales for a company with $15 million in annual sales.

The biggest change came in 1980 when we decided to move to Nova Scotia. In the summers we had always tried to return to Digby, Nova Scotia, and visit with Dianne's parents. We always enjoyed it and liked Nova Scotia very much. Moving there is something we never regretted.

On the advice of my brother-in-law we had taken out a one-year mortgage. When mortgage rates more than doubled a year later and we had to renew at 23.25 %, it was a great struggle to make ends meet. To assist with family financing, Dianne decided to resume work outside the house, which helped, but was not enough when one of my employers went into receivership. Not only did I find myself without a job, but I also lost $7,000 in commissions. To save our necks we arranged with the bank to give us a time of grace with the mortgage payments and allow three months during which to sell our home. It was during the last week of the three-month period that there was a knock on the front door during the supper hour by a couple interested in purchasing our home. The following day they made an offer through our real estate agent and the deal was closed before we had to crawl back again to the bank for more mercy.

From the time we moved to Nova Scotia to the time of our conversion in late 1984 we were very much involved in the Catholic church. Even while living in Ontario, I was an Extraordinary Minister, which allowed me to hand out communion during Mass. As a lay reader, I often read the epistle and, as in my younger days, I was also a member of the church choir.

My activities did not stop there, and as a couple Dianne and I got involved in the marriage preparation course for young couples. We also were chosen as leaders for a day of enrichment, separately for men and women of the parish in which we lived. It was just prior to this "day of enrichment" that God revealed Himself to me, but I had no full knowledge yet of the deception and powers of this world. I had no idea, for instance, that for 38 years I had been subject, along with my family and everybody I knew, to another spirit that had nothing to do with the true and living God but had been separated from Him.

It would take at least another three years into our Conversion before we were fully able to understand the full meaning of the words written in John 15:19:

If you were of the world, the world would love his own: but because you are not of the world, but I have chosen you out of the world, therefore the world hates you.

1 John 5:4.

For whatsoever is born of God overcometh the world.

NATURAL	REPENT		SPIRITUAL
BORN IN SIN			BORN OF GOD
DEATH			LIFE

Conversion

By the time I was 38 years old I had already started to read the Bible on a daily basis. The words began to have true meaning for me and it became clearer to me each day that there was a God that I had not known before. Many times I would get up in the night and read the Bible. On the morning of November 24, 1984 (my birthday), my eyes fell on one verse that seemed to stand out like a picture on the wall. The words were burned on my heart and I even wrote them down, as I often did when God revealed things to me. The words came out of the Book of Acts and read: "You are my Son and today I have become your Father." That evening Dianne gave me a birthday card and when I opened it there was a deep silence. The words that Dianne had written in the card were the same words that God had burned on my heart that morning: You are my Son and today I have become your Father.

During the spring of 1985, when Dianne and I were conducting our respective "days of enrichment", we often would sit around in the evenings and talk about the things God was teaching me. Our children, Chris and Angela, would often be part of our conversations and I thank God for guiding us all, without division, in the same direction.

One of the first things that God revealed to me was the process of repentance. By natural birth I had been born in sin, through the sinful seed of my natural father, and had been under that spirit of darkness ever since my birth. No baptism in the Catholic church had ever changed that and I would soon learn the full impact of that and other deceptions.

In May of 1985, as quick as lightning and based on what God had revealed to us, we were set free from going to Sunday Mass. Even our daughter Angela, who was an altar girl at the time, had no problem with our decision to go to church no longer. It was Angela, only ten years old, who told us that the local priest used to be drunk as he said Mass on Sunday mornings. While Dianne and I were already aware of this, what we also knew (and Angela did not) was that he used to entertain young men who were given weekend leave from prison. He had been a prison chaplain for ten years prior to his posting in our parish and it did not take long for rumors to spread through the community. We met him once, after we had left his congregation, while we were walking through a shopping mall. He informed us then that if we wanted to come back the door would be always open. We told him that we would never return as God had opened our eyes to the truth and had set us free for good. He died a few years later.

As soon as people in our community learned that we no longer would be attending church, it was as if all the armies of hell were coming after us. They used to come to our home to inquire what happened, or they would call us. As we were steadfast in our freedom and to what God had revealed to us, we ignored them. Dianne would not even answer the door, as they would often appear when I was not at home. We were only babes in our faith and it took many years of prayer and fasting before we were strong enough to confront the people of this world.

God really manifested Himself during one of my fasts. I often would fast, since it was the only effective way to deal with my physical affliction. When I fasted I felt strong and was able to deal with my affliction more effectively. Fasting for me had become a normal routine and my family had become accustomed to it. But when I fasted for six weeks one time, and only drank an occasional cup of tea or hot chocolate, we knew that it was a true manifestation from God and that He had sustained me. During this time of fasting I performed my normal daily duties, went to work every day but never lost any weight.

Often we hear of people who go on a hunger strike for some silly cause, only to find out that they have to be admitted into a hospital after only a few weeks because of weakness.

The true and living God truly has power over all flesh and the human body.

Matt 13:14,15

And in them is fulfilled the prophecy of Esaias, which saith, By hearing ye shall hear, and shall not understand; and seeing ye shall see, and shall not perceive: For this people's heart is waxed gross, and their ears are dull of hearing, and their eyes they have closed; lest at any time they should see with their eyes, and hear with their ears, and should understand with their heart, and should be converted, and I should heal them.

NATURAL	REPENT	SPIRITUAL
BORN IN SIN		BORN OF GOD
DEATH		LIFE

Repent

The Repentance process is very difficult to explain as it is a lifetime experience. Once God reveals what spirit controlled you from the time of your natural birth, you will wrestle with that spirit, while you dwell in this body. You need the living God each and every day of your life. He is the only One who can help you overcome that spirit. This is why the believers (the true church) offer themselves up to God each and every day for the renewing and transformation of their minds (Rom 12:1-2).

I would like to use the conversion of Paul as the basis of this chapter. When Jesus spoke to Paul he used the following words as written in Acts 26:16-18:

But rise and stand upon thy feet: for I have appeared unto thee for this purpose, to make thee a minister and a witness both of these things which thou hast seen, and of those things in the which I will appear unto thee; Delivering thee from the people, and from the Gentiles, unto whom now I send thee, To open their eyes, and to turn them from darkness to light, and from the power of Satan unto God, that they may receive forgiveness of sins, and inheritance among them which are sanctified by faith that is in me.

The above clearly explains the state of mankind. It

shows how mankind is blinded and that it lives in darkness and under the power of Satan.

The word repent used in the New Testament comes from the Greek word "metanoeo". It means: to change, transform, to think differently or reconsider. Please keep this in mind as you read the rest of this chapter.

In order to put the process of "Repentance" into words, we compiled the following guide. It will help if you allow yourself to be instructed by the words of the Bible.

In order to hear (John 9:31), understand (Eph 1:17-18), and live in union with the living God (John 10:16), mankind must repent (change) and be converted (Acts 3:19; Luke 3:13, 13:5, 15:10; 2 Tim 2:25-26). For a person to be transformed (Rom 12:2) from the spirit of darkness to the Spirit of light (Rom 7:25), he/she must first acknowledge that he/she is a sinner and that he/she lives under the power thereof (Matt 9:13; Mark 2:17; 1 John 1:8).

When a person acknowledges that he/she is a sinner, he/she must admit to the following:

By nature were you born in sin? The answer is yes.

Who is the father of sin? The answer is Satan.

By nature who is your father? The answer again is Satan.

Your natural spirit is referred to in the Bible as the devil, which all of mankind is born with.

Most people will stop right here as they will close their mind as soon as someone uses the word Satan or the devil. But Satan is real and empowers this whole world as he is the father of every man, woman and child. The problem is that there have been many organizations and religions that have used the word Satan and devil in their teachings but not in truth.

If you cannot acknowledge to the above in truth, there is no hope, as you will never know the difference between good and evil. You will die in your present state, which is sinful (Eze 18:20; Rom 6:23; 8:5-8; James 2:26) and under the power of the devil. It will be almost impossible for anyone to acknowledge to the above (Matt 19:26; Mark 10:27; Luke 18:27) if you are in bondage to any man-made religion or institution (Matt 15:9). Through the stronghold of religion (2 Cor 10:4; 2 Thess 2:11) all of mankind has been deceived and made to believe that they live in union with God. In truth they live in sin, according to the flesh, separated from God and under the power of sin (1 Cor 1:14), referred to as the spirit of darkness or the devil, which works through the flesh (1 Cor 1:29; Rom 8:8).

So, while the spirit of this world (Satan) has made you believe that you are a child of God, in truth you are under the power of sin and the devil. This is how Satan has transformed himself into an angel of light (2 Cor 11:14).

But thanks be to God my Father, for we no longer have to live according to the flesh and under the power of sin (please remember now who by nature your father is). To all those that turn to God in truth, He will reveal Himself through Jesus Christ and destroy the workings of the devil (your natural state) and free you from the power of sin (1 John 3:8-9).

Once you submit to serve the true and living God and commit yourself to follow in the footsteps of Jesus Christ, He will start to lead you to **REPENTANCE or**

the changing of spirits (2 Tim 2:25-26). He will teach you in all His ways (John 6:45; 14:26), and He will help you to overcome the spirit of this world and the workings of the flesh (Rom 7:25; 12:21; 1 Cor 15:57; 1 John 2:13-14; 4:4; 5:4-5; Rev 2:7, 11, 17, 26; 3:5,12,21; 12:11; 21:7). He will reveal Himself through Jesus Christ to you (Luke 10:21-22; John 8:19; Gal 1:16), and above all, He will open your eyes (Isa 42:7) to a new and better world - His Glorious Kingdom (Col 1:12-13).

Some of you may have walked to the infield of a Billy Graham Crusade or walked to the front of one of your churches to turn your life over to God. Through the process of Repentance, God will reveal to you that this has all been a misconception and a lie (John 8:44; Rom 3:4). If that is all you have to do, there would have been no need for Christ to come in the flesh.

Once, I myself was blind but now I can see. For more information how to become Born of God we encourage you to keep reading this book with an open heart.

We also encourage you to continue to study all of the Scriptural references in truth, for it is not me that speaks but the Spirit of my Father in heaven. As your Bible we suggest you use the authorized King James Version. Throughout the history of the Bible most translations became distorted as a result of ignorant men of this world (2 Cor 2:11; 2 Peter 1:20; Rev 22:18-19).

JOHN 13:20

VERILY, VERILY, I SAY UNTO YOU, HE THAT RECEIVETH WHOMSOEVER I SEND RECEIVETH ME; AND HE THAT RECEIVETH ME RECEIVETH HIM THAT SENT ME.

NATURAL	REPENT		SPIRITUAL
BORN IN SIN			BORN OF GOD
DEATH			LIFE

Born of God

As just about everybody in the religious community claimed him or herself to be "Born of God", it became clear to us that they had all been deceived. As we started to share our writings with people about being "Born of God" and what that meant, we were met with derision and disbelief. From these reactions we learned that what we share here is mature knowledge and only for those who have matured in the faith. It is what is referred to in the Bible as strong meat.

We learned that, when people turn to God and start the journey of repentance, they experience a total new beginning. They start as babies and little children on a new and narrow path. This is how the journey had started for us and we had to be careful how we shared this information, as it was hard to understand for anyone that was new in the faith.

It takes many years of hard work to reach maturity. Like a seed that falls to the ground, the old plant dies and a new one sprouts up. How quickly the new plant (the converted person) grows depends on the effort the individual puts into it.

ANYONE "BORN OF GOD" KNOWS THAT:

- This present world is Satan's kingdom (Luke 4:6; 11:18; John 12:31; 14:30; 2 Cor 4:4; Eph 2:2).

- To REPENT means to turn from darkness to light and from the power of Satan unto God (Eze 11:19; 36:26,27; Acts 26:18).

- To REPENT means to overcome the workings of Satan and the spirit of this world (Luke 13:1-5; 1 John 3:9; 5:4,18).

- By nature the devil does with every man at his will (Luke 4:6; 2 Tim 2:26).

- By nature you are not a child of God but a child of the devil (Eph 2:3; 1 John 3:10) and under the power of Satan (sin). Unless you turn to God and REPENT you will never understand the word of God (John 8:43-47) and you will die in your sin (Rom 6:23).

- Homosexuality and lesbianism is a punishment from God as a result of the unbelief of the nations (Rom 1:21-32).

- AIDS, cancer and every other disease is a punishment from God as a result of the unbelief of the nations (Ex 15:26; Deut 7:15).

- Earthquakes, famine and all other tragedies and disasters are a punishment from God as a result of the unbelief of the nations (Matt 24:7; Mark 13:8; Luke 21:11).

- Those who are mentally ill, handicapped, deaf or blind have an unclean spirit (devil) and that only faith in the true and living God would make them whole (Matt 9:6,29,32; 12:22; Mark 7:35; Luke 8:48; 17:19).

- If you had faith in the living God you would be healed from all your diseases (Matt 8:7; 10:8).

- Hospitals and the medical profession are a stronghold of Satan (2 Cor 10:4).

- Approximately 90% of all Canadians claiming to be Christians today have all been deceived by means of religious institutions. The Catholic church being the mother of them all (Rev 17:5).

- Every religious institution is a stronghold of Satan's divided kingdom (Matt 15:7-9; Mark 7:6-8; Luke 11:17,18) through which all the nations have been made drunk and have become spiritually blind (John 3:19; 12:40; 1 Cor 2:14, Rev 17:2).

- Satan deceives the whole world (Rev 12:9) and if you are a member of any religious institution or association, you too have been deceived by the spirit of this world (2 Cor 4:4). Because you say you can see, you have been made blind (John 9:39).

- The following people have transformed themselves (2 Cor 11:13) into the apostles of Christ: the Pope, Mother Theresa, Billy Graham, Jimmy Swaggert, Jerry Falwell, Rober Schuller, David Mainse, James Robison, your bishops, priests, deacons, pastors and ministers, etc., etc. (Matt 7:15; 24:23,24; 2 Cor 11:13,14).

- The above people represent a man-made image of a false Christ (Matt 24:24). They were not sent by God, neither did he command them. They speak to you a false vision and the deceit of their hearts (Jer 14:14) and through their preaching they have made the word of God of no effect (Gal 1:8,9; 1 Cor 1:17).

- By nature, the above people were born in sin and are under the power and servants thereof (John 8:34) and unless they REPENT and become born again (John 3:5-7) they will die in their sin (Rom 6:23).

- Sin is not just an act such as prostitution, alcoholism, adultery or a drug addiction, as the spirit of this world has made you believe, but is the fruit of every man, woman and child (Rom 3:9; Gal 3:22).

- The pro-life organization and its related abortion issue, child adoption, blood or organ donation, organ transplants, soup kitchens, food banks or any fund raising event has nothing to do with the gift of "LIFE" (John 4:14; 5:26; 6:27,35,54; 10:28; 17:3; Rom 2:7; 6:23; 1 John 1:2; 2:25; Rev 2:7,26).

- The mind of the natural man, this includes professors, scientists and theologians, is enmity with God (Rom 8:6,7) and that friendship with this world is enmity with God also (Rom 12:2; 2 Cor 6:17, Jas 4:4; 1 John 2:15).

- God cannot be received by this present world and that so-called world evangelization (global unity) is a deception at the highest level and the workings of the spirit of this world (John 1:5,10; 8:23; 14:17,22; 15:19,20; 17:9,14,16,25; 18:36: Rom 8:7; 1 Cor 1:20; 2:4-8, 12-14; 1 Thess 3:3; 2 Tim 3:12; Jas 4:4; 1 John 2:15; 3:1; 5:4,19; 2 John 7).

- Someday, at a time only known by God, Jesus Christ will return with all His saints (the believers) to do away with the workings of Satan, and to set up God's everlasting Kingdom (Matt 24:27; Acts 1:11; 1 Thess 4:15,16; Rev 20:2).

- The believers are few in number (Matt 7:14; 20:16; Luke 13:23) and, if it were possible, even the very elect would be deceived (Matt 24:24).

- Judges and lawyers (Luke 11:46-52) have no right to use the word of God in the courtrooms of the nations, for the word is God. It is truth and is not to be discerned (Hebr 4:12) or to be interpreted by any man (2 Peter 1:20). No man is to swear by the Bible (Lev 19:12; Jas 5:12).

- My doctrine is not of myself but of Him that sent me (John 7:16-18).

- I do not speak according to the wisdom of this world, but I speak the wisdom of God in a mystery (1 Cor 2:6-8).

- The sons of God have come for the pulling down of strongholds (Luke 11:21-23; 2 Cor 10:4).

- If you believed and turned (repented) from darkness to light and from the power of Satan unto God (Acts 26:18), God would lead you to repentance and show you the narrow way that leads to His Kingdom and to everlasting life (Matt 7:14; Mark 1:15).

- If you don't know what it means to believe in Jesus Christ and would like to receive the kingdom of God and the Gospel in truth, which can lead to repentance and remission of sin (Luke 24:47), we invite you start searching for the truth (Luke 14:16-24).

THE GIFT OF "LIFE" AND THE KNOWLEDGE TO THE MYSTERY OF THE KINGDOM (MARK 4:11) IS A FREE GIFT TO ALL THOSE THAT BELIEVE IN THE TRUTH (MATT 6:26; 10:8).

Matt 11:6   **Blessed is he, whosoever shall not be offended in me.**

Matt 9:13   **For I am not come to call the righteous, but sinners to repentance.**

Luke 13:3,5 **Except ye repent, ye shall all likewise perish.**

Luke 24:47   **And that repentance and remission of sins should be preached in His name among all nations, beginning at Jerusalem.**

1 John 1:8   **If we say we have no sin (that we are not under the power of Satan), we deceive ourselves, and the truth is not in us.**

2 John 7   **For many deceivers are entered into the world, who confess not that Jesus Christ is come in the flesh. This is a deceiver and an antichrist.**

Gal 1:10   **Do I seek to please man? For if it yet pleased men, I should not be the servant of Christ.**

LUKE 15:10

**THERE IS JOY IN THE PRESENCE
OF THE ANGELS OF GOD OVER
ONE SINNER THAT REPENTS.**

1 JOHN 4:6

**HE THAT KNOWETH GOD HEARETH US;
HE THAT IS NOT OF GOD HEARETH NOT US.**

Col 1:26,27

Even the mystery which hath been hid from ages and from generations, but now is made manifest to his saints: To whom God would make known what is the riches of the glory of this mystery among the Gentiles; which is Christ in you, the hope of glory.

NATURAL	REPENT		SPIRITUAL
BORN IN SIN			BORN OF GOD
DEATH			LIFE

The Mystery Babylon

As Dianne and I grew in our faith, everything became clear and easy to understand. It was as clear as looking into a mirror. God even directed us to those historical events and facts that proved how deception had entered into the world. Chapter 17 in the Book of Revelation clearly explains the facts surrounding the Mystery, Babylon the Great as mentioned in Rev 17:5. All of the historical facts explained and confirmed what God had already revealed to us.

On June 3, 1991, our local paper talked about the cardinals of the Catholic church being referred to by the Pope as "the princes of the church". In 1 Cor. 2:8 we read: which none of the princes of this world knew, for had they known it, they would not have crucified the Lord of glory. On May 30, 1991, it had also referred to "the cardinals as the red-hatted princes of the Roman Catholic Church".

In Revelation, chapter 17, it also talks about the woman sitting on the seven hills, referring thus to a false church. Is it not coincidence, then, that Rome is the only city that has been built on seven hills? The same chapter makes also reference to the colors "purple and scarlet". Has anyone ever noticed what the predominant color is when the hierarchy of the Catholic church gathers?

Revelation 17:4: "And the woman was arrayed in purple and scarlet color, and decked with gold and precious stones and pearls, having a golden cup in her hand full of abominations and filthiness and her fornication." This, I believe is a direct reference to the false church.

Isn't it a coincidence that the words "gold and precious stones" in Revelation 17:4, were repeated in 1991 (almost 2000 years after they were written) in an article in an international magazine to describe the golden chalice presented to Pope Pius IX.

The articles on the Mystery Babylon, Christmas and Easter in the next few chapters are based on historical facts alone. To accept them as official doctrines for salvation would be wrong.

Just because a person is not a member of the Catholic institution or any other so-called church, or does not celebrate Christmas or Easter, does not mean that that a person is saved or Born of God.

To the believers, the chapters on The Mystery Babylon, Christmas and Easter are merely a confirmation of how deception has entered into the world, while to the unbelievers it is merely a stumbling block, as is all of the Scriptures (1 Cor 1:23; 1 Peter 2:7,8).

The next time you visit your local bookstore, for example, I suggest you visit the world history or religious section. You will be able to find there many books that reveal the history of the religions of this world. You will also be able to find many books outlining the history of the Inquisition.

Many of them describe in explicit detail the history of the hundreds of years of cruelty and torture bestowed on mankind and as directed and ordered by the Vatican. Again, books like that only describe the historical events. But to the believers they also confirm how Satan has deceived this whole world (Rev 12:9).

The Spreading of the Babylonian Cult

Babylon was the seat of the great apostasy against God after the flood. It was here that the Babylonian cult was instituted by Nimrod and his queen Semiramis (Semiramis was Nimrod's mother and later his wife – in an incestuous relationship).

From the Babylonian cult is derived all types and forms of worship, carried over today into various pagan religions.

The Babylonian cult was a system claiming the highest wisdom and ability to reveal divine secrets. It was characterized by the word "mystery" because of its systems of claimed mysteries.

Besides confessing to a priest at admission, one was compelled to drink of "mysterious beverages" which was a requirement for those who sought initiation into these mysteries. Once admitted into the Babylonian mystery religion, men were no longer Babylonians, Assyrians or Egyptians, but became members of a mystical brotherhood over which was placed a supreme pontiff (or high priest) whose word was final in all matters. It was therefore a supranational organization. The object of the cult was to rule the world through its dogma.

This Babylonian system was one through which Satan planned to circumvent and defeat the truth of God. From Babylon it spread to the ends of the earth until, Scripture records, Abraham was chosen of God to flee these idolatrous nations and thus preserve the truth of God. Babylon continued to be the seat of worldwide satanic activity until it was conquered by Xerxes, King of Persia, in 487 BC, when the Babylonian priesthood (the Chaldeans) were forced to move to Pergamos, which then became their headquarters.

Over the years this cult gained power to the point that the Caesars absorbed the bulk of their principles and structure into their own pagan religion. Julius Caesar was made supreme pontiff of the Etruscan order in 74 BC thus establishing Babylon as the religion of Rome.

The Roman Emperors continued to hold this office until the year 376 AD when the Emperor Gratian, through Christian motivation, banned it when he saw that Babylonianism was idolatrous by nature. Religious matters then became somewhat disorganized until those in power decided once again to reestablish this position of apostasy.

In 378 AD, Damasus, bishop of Rome, was elected the Pontifex Maximus, the official high priest of the mysteries. This was brought about through the influence of the monks of Mount Carmel, a college of the Babylonian religion founded by the priest Jezebel and, incredibly, still in existence today within the Roman church. Since Rome was considered the most important city in the world, some of those who called themselves Christians looked to the bishop of Rome as "bishop of bishops" and head of the church. By this time, and through the years that followed, the streams of paganism and Christianity flowed together, producing what is known as the Roman Catholic Church, under the headship of the Pontifex Maximus, the Pope.

So in 378 AD the Babylonian system of religion became an official part of what they called the Christian church as it was then constituted. The bishop of Rome, who later became the supreme head of the Roman church was already supreme pontiff of the Babylonian order.

All the teachings of pagan Babylon and Rome were gradually absorbed into this so-called Christian religious organization. Soon after Damasus was made pontiff, the rites of Babylon began to come to the forefront.

The structure of worship of the Roman Catholic church became Babylonian and, under Damasus, heathen temples were restored and re-established.

The Roman church of today is purely a human institution. Its doctrines, which stand in opposition to God's word, were never taught by Christ or the apostles. They crept in over a long period of time.

I think it is clear, to anyone who examines the record, that Babylonian rites and practices were inserted into the Roman Catholic church when the supreme pontiff of the Babylonian order became its major influence. Many of today's pagan elements within the Catholic church were taken directly from the Babylonian religion as founded by Nimrod and Semiramis.

Pagan Rituals

- Worship of saints and the Virgin Mary.
- Private confession to a priest.
- The worship and veneration of images.
- The rosary.
- Monks and nuns.
- The sign of the cross. The sign had its origin in the mystic "Tau" of the Babylonian cult. This came from the letter T – the initial letter of Tammuz (Eze 8:14), but better known in classical writings and even today as Bacchus. Bacchus was also known as the lamented one. Actually, this was just one more name for Nimrod, the son of Cush.

Even today, Bacchus lives on as "the patron saint" of such disgusting homosexual orgies as are evident during the New Orleans Mardi Gras. Just about all the outstanding festivals, such as Christmas, Easter, Lent, St. John's Day, Lady Day, etc., are Babylonian in origin and have been adopted (after application of a thin veneer of Christianity) into the Catholic church, despite the fact that they have no relation to Christ or the Bible.

Heresies

A heresy is an opinion or doctrine contrary to the dogma of the true church. Listed below is a compilation of current religious practices that stem directly from pagan sources. These various traditions have been inserted into so-called Christianity during a period of over 1800 years.

Many of these practices were observed and followed over the years, but only at the times that they were officially adopted by councils and then proclaimed by the Pope did they become binding on all Catholics everywhere. The following heresies have no part in doctrines of the Lord Jesus Christ.

1. Of all human inventions taught and practiced by the Roman Catholic Church which are contrary to the Bible, the most ancient are the prayers for the dead and the sign of the cross. Both of these began about three hundred years after Christ and there is no mention of either within the Word of God.
2. Wax candles were introduced into churches about 320 AD. These votive candles supposedly help to bring about prayer requests when paid for and lit in conjunction with prayer.
3. Veneration of angels and saints began about 375 AD.
4. The mass, as a daily celebration, was adopted in 349 AD.
5. The worship of Mary, the mother of Jesus, and the use of the term "Mother of God" as applied to her, originated about 381 AD. This was officially decreed in the Council of Ephasis in 431 AD.

6. Priests began to adopt distinctive costumes about 500 AD.
7. The doctrine of purgatory was first established by Pope Gregory the Great about 593 AD.
8. The Latin language, as the language of prayer and worship in the church, was imposed by Pope Gregory in 600 AD (since changed). The Bible teaches that we pray to God alone, in the name of Jesus (John 16:23). In the early church, prayers were never directed to Mary or to saints. This practice began in the Roman church about six hundred years after Christ.
9. The papacy is of pagan origin. The title of Pope (universal bishop) was first given to the bishop of Rome about 600 AD, stemming from the Babylonian Cult (as previously explained). Jesus did not appoint Peter to the headship of the apostles and, in fact, expressly forbade such a notion (Luke 22:24-26; Eph 1:22-23; Col 1:18; 1 Cor 3:11).
10. The kissing of the Pope's feet began in 709 AD. It had been a pagan custom to kiss the feet of emperors. The Word of God forbids such practices (Acts 10:25-26; Rev 19:10; 22:8-9).
11. The temporal power of the Popes began in 750 AD. Jesus expressly forbade such a practice and He Himself refused any worldly kingship (Matt 4:8-10,20; 25-28; John 18:36).
12. The worship of the cross, images, and relics were authorized in 787 AD. Such practices are termed idolatry in the Bible and are severely condemned (Exodus 20:2-6; Deut 27:15; Psalm 135:15).
13. Holy water (water mixed with a pinch of salt and blessed by a priest) was authorized in 850 AD.
14. The canonization (official certification) of saints was instituted by Pope John XV in 995 AD. In the Bible,

every believer and follower of Christ is called "Saint" (Rom 1:7; 1 Cor 1:2 and many more).

15. The mass was developed gradually as a sacrifice (of Christ on the cross) and was obligatory in the eleventh century. (The Bible teaches that the sacrifice of Christ was offered once and for all and is not to be repeated, but only commemorated in the Lord's Supper (Hebr 7:27; 9:26-28; 10:10-14).

16. The celibacy of the priesthood was decreed by Pope Hildebrand Gregory VII in the year 1079 AD. Jesus imposed no such rules nor did any of the apostles. On the contrary, Peter was married and Paul states that bishops were to have one wife and could have children (1 Tim 3:5,12; Matt 8:14-15).

17. The rosary (or prayer beads) was introduced by Peter the Hermit in 1090 AD. This was copied from the Hindus and Mohammedans. The counting of prayers is a pagan practice and is expressly condemned by Christ (Matt 6:5-7).

18. The inquisition (torture) of heretics (anyone disagreeing with the interpretation coming out of Rome) was introduced by the Council of Verona in 1184 AD. (Jesus never taught the use of force to spread His Gospel).

19. The sale of indulgences (generally regarded as the purchase of forgiveness – for self or for deceased relatives – and a "permit" for indulging in sin) began in 1190 AD. The Christian religion, as taught in the Bible, condemns such, and it was primarily protest against this specific abuse that brought on the Protestant Reformation in the sixteenth century.

20. The dogma of transubstantiation was decreed by Pope Innocent III in 1215 AD. According to this doctrine, the priest miraculously changes the communion

wafer into the actual body of Christ – which he then proceeds to eat before the congregation. The Gospel condemns such superstitious absurdities. The act of Holy Communion is clearly a memorial observation of the sacrifice of Christ (Luke 22:19-20; John 6:35; 1 Cor 11:26).

21. The confession of sins to a priest at least once a year was instituted by Pope Innocent III in 1215 AD. (The Bible commands us to confess our sins directly to God: Psalm 51; Isa 1:18; Luke 7:48; 15:21; 1 John 1:8-9).

22. The adoration of the wafer ("the host") was invented by Pope Honorius in 1220 AD. (The Roman Catholic institution thus worships a god made by hands. This is, by Scriptural definition, idolatry and absolutely contrary to the teachings and the spirit of the Gospel: John 4:24).

23. The Bible was labeled a forbidden book by the Catholic institution (as far as laymen were concerned), and was placed in the index of forbidden books by the Council of Toledo in 1229 AD. (Jesus and Paul commanded that the Scriptures should be read by all people: John 5:39; 2 Tim 3:15-17).

24. The scapular was invented by Simon Stock, an English monk in 1287 AD. (This is a piece of brown cloth with a picture of the Virgin sewn onto it and superstitiously believed to assure salvation, no matter the depth of one's depravity, if worn next to the skin). This is superstition and fetishism of the most degrading type.

25. The Creed was adopted by the first council of Nicene in 325 AD and was approved by the first council of Constantinople in 381 AD. In the west the Creed was first used in the mass at Toledo in 589 AD, on the occasion of the reconciliation of the Gothic Arians

with the Catholic church.

26. The 40 days to make ready for Easter was prescribed by the Nicene Council in 325 AD.

27. The Catholic church forbade the cup (as part of Holy Communion) by instituting communion via the host alone in the Council of Constance in 1414 AD. (The Gospel commands us to celebrate Holy Communion with bread and wine: Matt 26:27; 1 Cor 11:26-29).

28. The doctrine of purgatory was proclaimed as a doctrine of faith by the Council of Florence in 1439 AD. (There isn't one word in the whole Bible suggesting that such a place as purgatory exists. Acceptance of the teachings and the blood of Jesus completely cleanses one of sin and leaves no sinful residue that must be burned off before we may enter the Kingdom: 1 John 1:7-9; 2:1-2; John 5:23; Rom 8:1).

29. The doctrine of seven sacraments was affirmed in 1439 AD. (The Gospel says that Christ instituted two sacraments – water baptism and the Lord's supper: Matt 28:19-20; 26:26-28).

30. The Council of Trent, held in 1545 AD (covering several years), declared tradition to be of equal authority with the Bible (by tradition is meant human opinions and the teaching of the same). There can never be any room for establishing traditions in opposition to Scripture. The Roman church is saying, in this doctrine, that when it chooses it can do anything it wishes in opposition to Scripture, and is in no way bound to Scripture. The Pharisees also believed this, and Jesus condemned them with no room for misunderstanding because of their position on this issue (Mark 7:7-13; Col 2:8; Rev 22:18).

31. The Immaculate Conception of the virgin Mary was proclaimed by Pope Pius IX in 1854 AD. This doc-

trine has nothing to do with Mary's conception of Jesus by the Holy Spirit. It says instead, that Mary was the only human ever born (except Adam and Jesus) without original sin. This implies therefore, that Mary did not need a Savior, and that she was divine. (The Gospel states, however, that all men (with the exception of Christ) are sinners. Mary herself states that she had need of a Savior, in that she refers to Christ as her Savior: Rom 3:23; 5:12; Psalm 51:5; Luke 1:30; 46-47).

32. In 1931, Pope Pius XI reaffirmed the doctrine that Mary is "the Mother of God" (a doctrine first decreed by the Council of Ephasus in the year 431. This is a heretical statement contrary to Mary's own words: Luke 1:46-47). The overwhelming percentage of the rites and ceremonies of the Roman church, such as temples, incense, oil lamps, votive offerings, holy water, holidays and seasons of devotions, processions, blessings of fields, homes and ships, sacerdotal vestments, the tonsures of priests, monks and nuns and images are all of pagan origin.

In Conclusion

The true church of believers (saints) is in Scripture referred to as a woman, a virgin woman, as a symbol of holiness and purity.

It is, as Scripture records, without spot (Eph 5:27; 2 Peter 3:14). Its offspring is referred to as the daughter of Zion and many other names.

The head of the false church is referred to as the Mystery Babylon or the mother of harlots (Catholic church), and any offspring is referred to as a harlot (other religions).

Any relationship with a harlot (false church) is called spiritual adultery, while the worshipping of idols and false images is often referred to as spiritual fornication. Scripture teaches us the following in 2 Cor 6:17: "Wherefore come out from among them, and touch not the unclean thing: and I will receive you."

Also, in Revelation 18:4 it says: "Come out of her, my people, that ye be not partakers of her sins, and that ye receive not of her plagues."

In order to receive a better understanding of the Mystery Babylon, mother of harlots, spiritual adultery and fornication, please read Revelation, chapters 17 and 18.

Spiritual Fornication (worshipping of idols): Numbers 25:1-5; 1 Cor 5:9-10, 6:9; 10:7-8

Spiritual Adultery (joined to a harlot or a false church): Jer 3:1-9; 13:27; Eze 16:15-26; Hosea 2-5; 3:3; 4:14-15; 1 Cor 6:13-16 and Rev 2:22.

NATURAL	REPENT		SPIRITUAL
BORN IN SIN			BORN OF GOD
DEATH			LIFE

Popes and the Princes of this World

Nowhere in the book of Acts, which is the most complete history of the Early Church (group of believers), is there any suggestion of the position of Pope.

Only gradually did the concept of an organized church – governed, directed, and regulated by a hierarchy of popes, bishops and priests – evolve. And even then, it did so despite widespread opposition.

It was Cyprian, bishop of Carthage (who died in 258 AD) who introduced the concepts that were to bring revolutionary changes in worship patterns within the church. Cyprian claimed that the bishop of Rome derived his authority directly from God and should therefore, be obeyed by all people.

In the years following, this concept was gradually introduced into existing practice, and church government eventually became almost completely autocratic. Believers in the truth, even in those days, were persecuted and murdered for their faith.

During the years 440 AD to 461 AD, Leo I, as the bishop of Rome, used all his considerable powers to establish recognition for the bishop of Rome as "the universal bishop", having universal power over the Roman church. It was he who first made the claim that Peter had been the first pope. Leo's claim was enforced through the power of the Roman Emperor, but received only marginal acceptance within the church.

Even the Council of Chalcedon, where Leo exercised great power, refused his request to certify his claims. His assertions of papal supremacy did, however, produce a profound effect in later years, although the doctrine of papal infallibility was not officially declared until 1970.

Facts

- Leo I (440-461 AD) advocated the death penalty for heresy.

- Leo II (682-683 AD) pronounced one of his predecessors, Pope Honorius I, a heretic.

- Stephen II (752-757 AD) encouraged the military conquest of Italy by Pepin, and accepted the lands as papal property.

- Sergius III (904-911 AD) had a mistress, and their illegitimate offspring subsequently became pope.

- John X (914-928 AD) had multiple mistresses and was killed in the physical act of adultery by an irate husband.

- Boniface VII (984-985 AD) murdered his predecessor, John XIV.

- Boniface VIII (1294-1303 AD) bought his papacy.

- Benedict IX (1033-1045AD) was made pope at the age of 12. He committed public murders and robberies and was driven out of Rome.

- Pope Innocent VIII (1484-1492 AD) was the father of sixteen children by various women. What ever happened to the vow of celibacy?

Such transgressions as adultery, sodomy, simony, rape, murder, drunkenness and incest are among the iniquities that have been committed by Popes.

In 1045 and 1046 there were three rival popes. During the reign of Alexander III (1159-1181 AD) there were four rival popes. At times the papal office was obtained through murder and bribery. To link such an office with men who have claimed to be the "Holy Father", the "Vicar of Christ" and Bishop of bishops may sound shocking, but this is still the claim they make today. In truth, it is just another way in which Satan has transformed himself into an angel of light.

The incredible cruelty of the inquisition was initiated by Pope Innocent III (1198-1216 AD) and was to last for 500 years. This was a court whose purpose was to root out and punish heretics. The lands and properties of condemned heretics became the property of the Catholic church. It served two practical purposes – dissenters who disagreed with Catholic doctrines were silenced and the pope's coffers were expanded.

People of all faiths were horribly tortured, tested, and tried during those centuries. Pope Innocent IV issued an official document, which stated that heretics – those who would not bow to the Roman system – were to be crushed like venomous snakes. His soldiers were promised property and remission of all their sins if they killed a heretic. Victims of the inquisition were stretched and torn apart on the "rack". Some were crushed and stabbed to death in the "iron virgin". There was the thumb-screw, an instrument made for disarticulating the fingers and "Spanish Boots" which were used to crush the legs and feet. Pincers were used to tear out fingernails or were applied red-hot to the sensitive parts of the body.

Every imaginable method of torture was used that fiendish men could imagine. Those who wouldn't bow to the Pope's system were shut up in caves and dungeons, nailed to trees, tormented with fires, scalded with oil or burning pitch; or melted lead was poured into their eyes, ears and mouths. They were also scalped, skinned, flayed alive; heads were twisted off and eyes gouged out; women were defiled, their breasts cut off; babies were brutally beaten, whipped, stabbed, dashed against trees – in front of their parents – then thrown to hungry dogs and swine. There are no official records of how many people were killed but estimates range from 25 to 50 million. Whatever the exact number, we know that millions were killed and murdered in the most hideous and cruel way during those dark ages by the persecutions that were promoted and directed by the papacy (Rev 17:6; 19:2).

Reading the above and considering the history of the Catholic church, it is no wonder that the Bible refers to it as a beast and a dragon.

It is even described as a **red** dragon and a **scarlet** colored beast. During major celebrations, in particular those involving cardinals, the predominant color is scarlet or red and this reference can also be found in the Bible. The Roman Catholic church also refers to its cardinals as **the princes of this world** and this reference is also found in the Bible. Let us first explore the use of the color red in the Bible.

Revelation 12:3.
And behold a great **red** dragon.

Revelation 17:3.
And I saw a woman (false church) sit upon a **scarlet** colored beast.

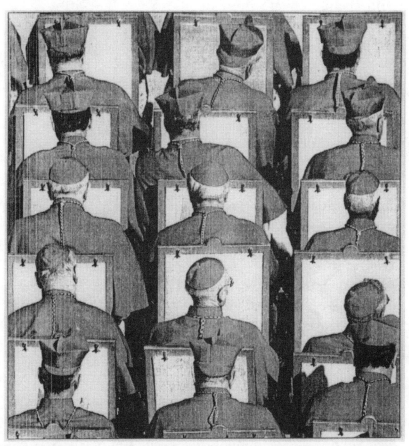

The above picture of newly appointed cardinals showed up in our local paper with the headline: "Church Princes Take Their Place". The bible refers to the princes of this world in 1 Cor 2:6-8. It is important to remember that a cardinal's most important job is to elect a new pope, who is chosen from their number, but not by God. The predominant color in the above picture is red / scarlet.

Revelation 17:4.

And the woman was arrayed in purple and **scarlet** colour.

When the Pope appointed 22 new cardinals a local paper reported on May 30, 1991:

"The new cardinals, **red** hatted **princes** of the Roman Catholic Church..."

The same year, on June 3rd, another paper wrote: "Cardinals are the Pope's closest advisers and, as **princes** of the church, his closest representatives around the world."

On February 22, 1998, a local paper headlined an article on the cardinals of the Catholic church as follows: "Church **princes** take their place."

Chalice made of "gold and precious stones" said to be taken from the trappings of a horse that a Turkish sultan presented to Pope Pius IX. It is no coincidence that the same words can be found in Revelation 17:4.

Let us turn now to 1 Cor 2:6-8 where we read:

"Howbeit we speak wisdom among them that are perfect: yet not the wisdom of this world, nor of the **princes** of this world, that come to nought: but we speak the wisdom of God in a mystery, even the hidden wisdom, which God ordained before the world unto our glory: which none of the **princes** of this world knew: for had they known it, they would not have crucified the Lord of glory."

Isn't it amazing how this world has been blinded for so long. Christ Himself spoke the following words in Matthew 10:26. "Fear them not therefore: for there is nothing covered, that shall not be revealed; and hid, that shall not be known."

Rev 17:4 also speaks about the woman (false church) being decked with **gold and precious stones** and pearls, having a golden cup in her hand full of abominations and filthiness of her fornication.

I have subscribed for many years to an international magazine. Many years ago it showed a picture of a golden chalice with the following inscription below:

Chalice made of gold and precious stones said to be taken from the trappings of a horse that a Turkish sultan presented to Pope Pius IX in the late 1800s. It is no coincidence that the same words were used to describe the picture of the chalice as you find in Revelation 17:4. Seek and you will find the truth for yourself (Matt 7:7).

Matt 15:13,14

Every plant, which my heavenly Father hath not planted, shall be rooted up. Let them alone: they be blind leaders of the blind. And if the blind lead the blind, both shall fall into the ditch.

NATURAL	REPENT	SPIRITUAL
BORN IN SIN		BORN OF GOD
DEATH		LIFE

Shroud of Turin a Hoax

For centuries people have worshipped the "Shroud of Turin" as the burial cloth of Christ, although it can be confirmed that it is a hoax, using the very words of Scripture.

Turning to John 11:44 we read the following: "And he (Lazarus) that was dead came forth, bound hand and foot with graveclothes; and his face was bound about with a napkin."

The word napkin comes from the Greek word "soudarion" which is a sweat cloth or towel used for wiping perspiration from the face or for binding the face of a corpse. We see here clearly that a separate cloth was used for the face.

When we read John 20: 6-7 we read the following: "Then cometh Simon Peter following him, and went into the sepulchre, and seeth the linen clothes lie, and the napkin, that was about his head, not lying with the linen clothes, but wrapped together in a place by itself."

We clearly see here that, not only was a separate cloth used for Christ's head, but that it was even placed in a different location.

This confirms that the Shroud of Turin – a single cloth measuring 14 feet, 3 inches\ by 3 feet, 7 inches, believed to have been used for the burial of Jesus Christ and bearing his features – is a hoax.

I am sure that many will wonder why for centuries

*Line drawing after the painting by Giulio Clovia of the
Body of Christ being prepared for burial. The Bible proves
that a separate cloth was used for Christ's head.*

this has remained such a mystery, since the Bible dis-
proves its very existence so clearly. In the following
readings you will find that the gospel of Jesus Christ,
and all the rest of Scripture, is a mystery to the natural man: Matt 13:35, Rom 16:25, 1 Cor 2:7,14, Eph 3:9
and Col 1:26.

This is the result of the sinful nature of mankind
and its choice to continue to live according to the spirit
and rudiments of this world, controlled by Satan, who is
the master of sin. For this reason all of mankind continues to be blinded and separated from the truth and the
Spirit of God (John 8:42-45; 1 John 3:8 and Rev 12:9).

For thirty-eight years, I myself walked in bondage
under the elements of this world (Gal 4:3), and did service unto them, which by nature are no gods (Gal 4:8).

Throughout the history of the Roman Church, the
Pope has claimed to preside over the Chair of Peter.
First of all, Peter was never a Pope. He was an apostle,

servant and a soldier for Christ. Some historians have said that he died in Rome by the hand of the Romans. Concerning the so-called "Chair of Peter", a scientific commission appointed by Pope Paul in July of 1968 has now reported that no part of the chair is old enough to date from the time of Peter. In the official report on the carbon dating and other tests, it has been determined that the chair is no older than the ninth century.

The above revelation (Eph 1:17 and Eph 3:3-5) is the first of many to this present world. This world will see (and already has) many manifestations of the Sons of God (Rom 8:19), before the glorious appearing of the Great God and our Savior Jesus Christ (Titus 2:13).

Many readers may find the things we write about rather controversial or even evil (1 Peter 2:12 and 1 Peter 3:16). However, as it is our wish that all mankind come to the true knowledge

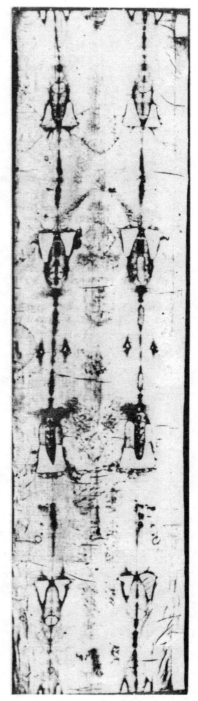

Positive image of the Shroud.

63

Negative image of the face on the Shroud.

of Jesus Christ, we ask that you will take the time to study all the scriptural references, so that your eyes may be opened to the truth also.

Be assured that the Sons of God have come to the pulling down of strongholds (2 Cor 10:4 and Matt 10:26-28), religion being the strongest of them all.

NATURAL	REPENT		SPIRITUAL
BORN IN SIN			BORN OF GOD
DEATH			LIFE

Christmas: Strictly a Pagan Celebration

December 25 is the day designated on our calendars as the day of Christ's birth. But is this really the day on which He was born? Are today's customs at this season of Christian origin? Or is Christmas another example of mixture between paganism and so-called Christianity?

A look at the word "Christmas" indicates that it is a mixture. Though it includes the name of Christ, it also mentions the "Mass". When we consider all of the elaborate ceremonies, prayers for the dead, transubstantiation rites, and complicated rituals of the Roman Catholic Mass, can any truly link this with the historical Jesus of the Gospels? His life and ministry were uncomplicated by such rituals. Like Paul, we fear that some have been corrupted "from the simplicity that is in Christ" (2 Cor 11:3) because of pagan influence upon such things as the Mass. Looking at it this way, the word "Christ-mas" is self-contradictory.

It is not essential that we know the exact date on which Christ was born, the main thing being, of course, that He was born! The early Christians remembered the death of Christ during the breaking of the bread (1 Cor 11:26), not His birth. The Catholic Encyclopedia says, "Christmas was not among the earliest festivals of the church." Irenaeus and Tertullian omit it from their lists of feasts. Later, when churches at various places did begin celebrating the birthday of Christ, there was much difference of opinion as to the correct date. It was not until the latter part of the fourth century that the Roman Church began observing December 25. Yet, by the fifth century, it was ordering that the birth of Christ be forever observed on this date, even though this was the day of the old Roman feast of the birth of Sol, one of the names of the sun-god!

Says Frazer in The Golden Bough: "The largest pagan religious cult which fostered the celebration of December 25 as a holiday throughout the Roman and Greek worlds was the pagan sun worship – Mithraism. This winter festival was called "The Nativity" – the Nativity of the Sun. Was this the pagan festival responsible for the December 25 day being chosen by the Roman Church? We will let The Catholic Encyclopedia answer. "The well-known solar feast of 'Natalis Invicti' – the Nativity of the Unconquered Sun – celebrated on December 25, has a strong claim on the responsibility for our December date."

As pagan solar customs were being christianized at Rome, it is understandable that confusion would result. Some thought Jesus was Sol, the sun-god! "Tertullian had to assert that Sol was not the Christian's God; Augustine denounced the heretical identification of Christ with Sol. Pope Leo I bitterly reproved solar survivals – Christians, on the very doorstep of the Apostles' basilica, turning to adore the rising sun."

The winter festival was very popular in ancient times: "In pagan Rome and Greece, in the days of the Teutonic barbarians, in the remote times of ancient Egyptian civilization, in the infancy of the race, East and West and North and South, the period of the winter solstice was ever a period of rejoicing and festivity." Because this season was so popular, it was adopted as the time of the birth of Christ by the Roman Church.

Some of our present-day Christmas customs were influenced by the Roman Saturnalia. "It is common knowledge", says one writer, "that much of our association with the Christmas season – the holidays, the giving of presents and the general feeling of geniality – is but the inheritance from the Roman winter festival of the Saturnalia ... survivals of paganism."

Tertullian mentions that the practice of exchanging presents was a part of Saturnalia. There is nothing wrong in giving presents, of course. The Israelites gave gifts to each other at times of celebration – even celebrations that were observed because of mere custom (Esther 9:22). But the church sought to link Christmas gifts with those presented to Jesus by the wise men. This cannot be correct. By the time the wise men arrived, Jesus was no longer "lying in a manger", but was in a house (Matt: 9-11). This could have been quite a while after his birthday. Also, they presented their gifts to Jesus, not to each other!

The Christmas tree, as we know it, only dates back a few centuries, though ideas about sacred trees are very ancient. An old Babylonish fable told of an evergreen tree which sprang out of a dead tree stump. The old stump symbolized the dead Nimrod, the new evergreen tree symbolized that Nimrod had come to life again in Tammuz. Among the Druids the oak was sacred, among the Egyptians it was the palm, and in Rome it was the fir, which was decorated with red berries during the Saturnalia. The Scandinavian god Odin was believed to bestow special gifts at yuletide to those who approached his sacred fir tree. In at least ten Biblical references, the green tree is associated with idolatry and false worship (1 Kings 14:23, etc). Since all trees are green at least part of the year, the special mention of "green" probably refers to trees that are evergreen. "The Christmas tree... recapitulates the idea of tree worship... gilded nuts and balls symbolize the sun... all of the festivities of the winter solstice have been absorbed into Christmas day... the use of holly and mistletoe from the Druid ceremonies; the Christmas tree from the honors paid to Odin's sacred fir."

Taking all of this into consideration, it is interesting to compare a statement of Jeremiah with today's customs of decorating a tree at the Christmas season. "The customs of the people are vain: for one cutteth a tree out of the forest, the work of the hands of the workman with the axe. They deck it with silver and with gold; they fasten it with nails and with hammers, that it move not. They are upright as the palm tree, but speak not" (Jer 10:3,4).

The people in the days of Jeremiah, as the context shows, were actually making an idol of the tree, the word "workman" being not merely a lumberjack, but one who formed idols (cf. Isaiah 40:19,20; Hosea 8:4-6). And the word "axe" refers here specifically to a carving tool.

In the sixth century, missionaries (false apostles) were sent through the northern part of Europe to gather pagans into the Roman fold. They found that June 24 was a very popular day among these people and sought to "Christianize" it. By this time December 25 had been adopted by the Roman church as the birthday of Christ. Since June 24 was approximately six months before December 25, why not call this the birthday of John the Baptist? John was born, it should be remembered, six months before Jesus (Luke 1:26,36). Thus June 24 is known on the papal calendar now as St. John's Day!

In Britain, before the adoption of "Christianity", June 24 was celebrated by the Druids with blazing fires in honor of Baal. Herodotus, Wilkinson, Layard, and other historians tell of these ceremonial fires in different countries. When June 24 became St. John's Day, the sacred fires were adopted also and became "St. John's fires". These are mentioned as such in the Catholic Encyclopedia. "I have seen the people running and leaping through the St. John's fires in Ireland," says a writer of the past century, "...proud of passing through unsinged ... thinking themselves in a special manner blest by the ceremony." It would seem that such rites would sooner honor Molech than John the Baptist!

June 24 was regarded as being sacred to the ancient fish god Oannes, a name by which Nimrod was known. In an article on Nimrod, Fausset says: "Oannes the fish god, Babylon's civilizer, rose out of the red sea..." In the Latin language of the Roman church, John was called JOANNES. Notice how similar this is to OANNES! Such similarities helped promote the mixture of paganism into "Christianity".

A day which in pagan times had been regarded as sacred to Isis and Diana, August 15, was simply renamed as the day of the "Assumption of the Virgin Mary" and right up to our present time is still highly honored. Another day adopted from paganism, supposedly to honor Mary, is called "Candlemas" or the "Purification of the Blessed Virgin" and is celebrated on February 2nd. In Mosaic Law, after giving birth to a male child, a mother was considered unclean for forty days (Lev 12). "And when the days of her purification according to the Law of Moses were accomplished", Joseph and Mary presented the baby Jesus in the temple and offered the prescribed sacrifice (Luke 2:22-24). Having adopted December 25 as the nativity of Christ, the February date seemed to fit in well with the time of purification of Mary. But what did this have to do with the use of candles on this day? In pagan Rome, this festival was observed by the carrying of torches and candles in honor of Februa, from whom our month February is named.

The Greeks held the feast in honor of the Goddess Ceres, the mother of Proserpina, who, with candle-bearing celebrants, searched for her in the underworld.

Thus we can see how adopting February 2nd to honor the purification of Mary was influenced by pagan customs involving candles, even to calling it "Candlemass" day. On this day, all of the candles to be used during the year in Catholic rituals are blessed. Says the Catholic Encyclopedia. "We need not shrink from admitting that candles, like incense and lustral water, were commonly employed in pagan worship and in rites paid to the dead."

If the apostle Paul were to preach to today's generation, we wonder if he would not say to the professing church, as he did to the Galatians long ago, "Ye observe days and months and times, and years, I am afraid of you, lest I bestowed upon you labor in vain" (Gal 4:9-11). The context shows that the Galatians had been converted from the pagan worship of "gods". When some had turned again to their former worship, the days and times they observed were evidently those which had been set aside to honor pagan gods! Later, strangely enough, some of these very days were merged into the worship of the "professing church" but, in truth, they have nothing to do whatsoever with the true church of saints, believers in the true and living God.

NATURAL	REPENT	SPIRITUAL
BORN IN SIN		BORN OF GOD
DEATH		LIFE

Easter: Strictly a Pagan Celebration

From where did Easter observance come? Did the early Christians dye Easter eggs? Did Peter or Paul ever conduct an Easter sunrise service? The answers, of course, are obvious.

The word "Easter" appears once in the King James Version: "... intending after Easter to bring Him forth to the people" (Acts 12:4). The word translated as "Easter" here is "pascha", which is – as all scholars know – the Greek word for passover and has no connection with the English "Easter". It is well known that Easter is not a Christian expression – not in its original meaning. The word comes from the name of a pagan goddess – the goddess of the rising light of day and spring. "Easter" is but a modern form of Eostre, Pstera, Astarte, or Ishtar, the latter, according to Hislop, being pronounced as we pronounce "Easter" today.

Like the word "Easter", many of our customs at this season had their beginnings among pagan religions. Easter eggs, for example, are colored, hid, hunted, and eaten – a custom done innocently today and often linked with a time of fun and frolic for children. But this custom did not originate in so-called Christianity. The egg was a sacred symbol among the Babylonians who believed an old fable about an egg of wondrous size which fell from heaven into the Euphrates River. From this marvelous egg – according to the ancient myth – the goddess Astarte (Easter) was hatched. The egg came to symbolize the goddess Easter.

The ancient Druids bore an egg as the sacred emblem of their idolatrous order. The procession of Ceres in Rome was preceded by an egg. In the mysteries of Bacchus an egg was consecrated. China used dyed or colored eggs in sacred festivals. In Japan, an ancient custom was to make the sacred egg a brazen color. In northern Europe, in pagan times, eggs were colored and used as symbols of the goddess of spring. Among the Egyptians, the egg was associated with the sun – the "golden egg". Their dyed eggs were used as sacred offerings at the Easter season.

Says Encyclopedia Britannica, "The egg as a symbol of fertility and of renewed life goes back to the ancient Egyptians and Persians, who had also the custom of coloring and eating eggs during their spring festival." How then, did this custom come to be associated with so-called Christianity? Apparently some sought to Christianize the egg by suggesting that, as the chick comes out of the egg, so Christ came out of the tomb. Pope Paul V (1605-1621) even appointed a prayer in this connection: "Bless, O Lord, we beseech thee, this thy creature of eggs, that it may become wholesome sustenance unto thy servants, eating it in remembrance of our Lord Jesus Christ."

The following quotations from the Catholic Encyclopedia are significant. "Because the use of eggs was forbidden during Lent, they were brought to the table on Easter Day, colored red to symbolize the Easter joy... The custom may have its origin in Paganism, for a great many customs celebrating the return of spring, gravitated to Easter"!

Such was the case with a custom that was popular in Europe. "The Easter fire is lit on top of mountains from new fire, drawn from wood by friction; this is a custom of pagan origin in vogue all over Europe, signifying the victory of spring over winter. The bishops issued severe edicts against sacrilegious Easter fires, but did not succeed in abolishing them everywhere." So what happened? Notice this carefully! "The church adopted the observance into the Easter ceremonies, referring to the fiery column in the desert and the resurrection of Christ!" Were pagan customs mixed into the Romish church and given the appearance of Christianity? It is not necessary to take my word for it, in numerous places the Catholic Encyclopedia comes right out and says so.

"Like the Easter egg," says the Encyclopedia Britannica, "the Easter hare came to Christianity from antiquity. The hare is associated with the moon in the legends of ancient Egypt and other peoples... Through the fact that the Egyptian word for hare, um, means also "open" and "period", the hare came to be associated with the idea of periodicity, both lunar and human, and with the beginning of new life in both the young man and young woman, and so a symbol of fertility and of the renewal of life. As such, the hare became linked with Easter... eggs." Finally, one more quote concerning the Easter rabbit: "The rabbit is a pagan symbol and has always been an emblem of fertility."

At the Easter season it is not uncommon for so-called Christians to attend sunrise services. It is assumed that these honor Christ because he rose from the dead on Easter Sunday morning, just as the sun was coming up. But the resurrection did not actually occur at sunrise, for it was still dark when Mary Magdalene came to the tomb and it was already empty!

Rites connected with the dawning sun have been known among many ancient nations in one form of another. In Egypt, the Sphinx was located so as to face the east. From Mount Fuji-yama, Japan, prayers are made to the rising sun. "The pilgrims pray to their rising sun while climbing the mountain sides... sometimes one may see several hundreds of Shinto pilgrims in their white robes turning out from their shelters, and joining their chants to the rising sun." The pagan Mithraists of Rome met together at dawn in honor of the sun-god.

The goddess of spring, from whose name our word "Easter" comes, was associated with the sun rising in the east – even as the very word "East-er" would seem to imply. Thus the dawn of the sun in the east, the name Easter, and the spring season are all connected.

According to the old legends, after Tammuz was slain, he descended into the underworld. But through the weeping of his "mother", Ishtar (Easter), he was mystically revived in spring. Says Smith in Man and his Gods: "The resurrection of Tammuz through Ishtar's grief was dramatically represented annually in order to insure the success of the crops and the fertility of the people.Each year, men and women had to grieve with Ishtar over the death of Tammuz and celebrate god's return in order to win anew her favor and her benefits."

When the new vegetation began to come forth, those ancient people believed their "Savior " had come from the underworld, had ended winter, and caused spring to begin. Even the Israelites adopted the doctrines and rites of the annual pagan spring festival, for Ezekiel speaks of "women weeping for Tammuz" (Eze 8:14).

As Christians, we believe that Jesus Christ rose from the dead in reality – not merely in nature or the new vegetation of spring. Because his resurrection was in the spring of the year, it was not too difficult for the "church" of the fourth century (now having departed from the original faith in a number of ways) to merge the pagan spring festival into so-called Christianity. In speaking of this merger, the Encyclopedia Britannica says, "Christianity... incorporated in its celebration of the great Christian feast day many of the heathen rites and customs of the spring festival."

Legend has it that Tammuz was killed by a wild boar when he was 40 years old. Hislop points out that 40 days – a day of each year Tammuz had lived on earth – were set aside to "weep for Tammuz". In olden times, these forty days were observed with weeping, fasting, and self-chastisement, to gain anew his favor so he would come forths from the underworld and cause spring to begin. This observance was not only known to Babylon, but also among the Phoenicians, Egyptians, Mexicans and, for a time, even among the Israelites. "Among the pagans," says Hislop, "this Lent seems to have been an indispensable preliminary to the great annual festival in commemoration of the death and resurrection of Tammuz."

Having adopted other beliefs about the spring festival into the Roman church, it was a natural step in the development to also adopt the old "fast" that preceded the festival. The Catholic Encyclopedia very honestly points out that "writers in the fourth century were prone to describe many practices (e.g., the Lenten fast of 40 days) as of Apostolic institution which certainly had no claim to be so regarded." It was not until the sixth century that the Pope officially ordered the observance of Lent, calling it a "sacred feast", during which people were to abstain from meat and a few other foods.

Catholic scholars know and recognize that there are customs within their church that were borrowed from paganism. But they reason that many things, though originally pagan, can be "Christianized". If some pagan tribe observed 40 days in honor of a pagan god, why should we not do the same, only in honor of Christ (false Christ)? Though pagans worshipped the sun towards the east, could we not have sunrise services to honor the resurrection of Christ, even though this was not the time of day He rose? Even though the egg was used by pagans, can't we continue its use and pretend that it symbolizes the large rock that was in front of the tomb? In other words, why not adopt all kinds of popular customs, only instead of using them to honor pagan gods, as the heathen did, use them to honor Christ?

It all sounds very logical, yet a much safer guideline is found in the Bible itself: "Take heed to thyself that thou not be snared by following them, after that they be destroyed from before thee; and that thou inquire not after their gods, saying: How did these nations serve their gods? Even so will I do likewise. Thou shalt not do so unto the Lord thy God: for every abomination to the Lord, which he hateth, have they done into their gods; for even their sons and their daughters they have burnt in the fire to their gods. What thing soever I command you, observe to do it; thou shalt not add thereto (Deut 12:30-32)."

It is obvious that the Easter celebration incorporated by the Roman church has nothing to do with the truth concerning the Lord Jesus Christ and the true church of the believers (saints).

NATURAL	REPENT	SPIRITUAL
BORN IN SIN		BORN OF GOD
DEATH		LIFE

Foundations Out of Course

Are all of the foundations of the earth out of course? When you read those words from Psalm 82:5, all you have to do is to read the editorial comments of people in the local newspapers on such issues as: religion, abortion, homosexuality, immorality, AIDS, etc.

Hundreds of people have written to their local newspapers in the last few years, condemning homosexuality only to have the Roman Catholic Archbishop of Westminster come out recently with words of praise towards homosexual friendship and love. Something must be drastically wrong when the views of a leader are so opposite to his followers. Something must be drastically wrong also when the leaders of denominational churches stand so vehemently in opposition to abortion, only to have a Canadian province like Quebec record more abortions than any other province, while the majority of its people are Roman Catholic. Or a country like Brazil, which is predominately Roman Catholic, but nevertheless records more abortions than any other country in the world.

On one side of the issue are those who support Pro-Life and on the other side those who support Pro-Choice, who also use the very words from the Bible ("judge and you will not be judged") to support their cause, just as do those who support Pro-Life.

Is it possible that perhaps both sides are wrong and that neither side understands the words from the Bible?

Is there a possibility that the Bible is true? Perhaps, the Pro-Life organization has nothing to do with the true gift of "Life" and the judgement of Pro-Choice is perhaps after the judgement of mankind (who judge after the flesh) and has nothing to do with the true judgement from God? Like everyone else, by nature they were born in sin and under the spirit of darkness and unless they repent they will die in their sin (Luke 13:1-5). As explained in chapters 5 and 6 of this book, sin is not just an act such as prostitution, alcoholism, adultery, a drug addiction or abortion, as the spirit of this world has made you believe, but it is the fruit of every man, woman and child (Rom 3:9; Gal 3:22).

Something must be drastically wrong when a bishop lectures his followers on issues like immorality, while at the same time a number of priests in his own diocese are convicted of sexual abuse involving young children. Something must be drastically wrong when the leaders of denominational churches talk about healing, while at the same time all of the hospitals are bursting at the seams and mankind continues to explore new ways to combat every imaginable disease.

Is there a possibility after all that the Bible is true when it says that all of the foundations of the earth are out of course? Is it possible that the Bible is true, when it speaks about the religious leaders being blind guides, who are misleading the people through their own doctrines? Is it possible that the Bible is right when it speaks about this whole world being deceived and that it is true when it speaks about "REPENTANCE" and the commitment to turn from darkness to light and from the power of Satan unto God (Acts 26:18)?

Is the Bible true about the natural man not being able to receive the things that are of God (1 Cor 2:14).

When most people claim to be children of God, could the Bible be true when it teaches that they have been deceived and that they are in fact the children of the devil (John 8:44)? Is it possible that the Bible is a deep hidden mystery, which few are able to understand (Col 1:26, Matt 7:14)?

Do the people of this world really know Christ or do they follow after a false Christ? Would they believe Him if He spoke to them in person or through one of His ministers?

After all, if He came to set His people free from the rudiments of this world, then why do they continue to follow after them?

If one were to seek the truth concerning the Bible, one would be able to clearly see for oneself, that the words in the Bible are true and that they are a discerner for every thought and issue in this life (Hebr 4:12). It will also prove that this whole world has been deceived, as stated in Rev 12:9, through man-made doctrines in which there is no solution or salvation.

Mankind has been given free will and because of this free will they will not accept the message concerning the true and living God. They would rather believe in a lie and continue to live in darkness and under the power of Satan. In a way mankind is like the ring-tailed monkey. For many years the Zulu tribe in Africa has been catching this agile little animal with ease using nothing more than a melon growing on a vine, the seeds of which are a favorite snack of the monkey's. The Zulus simply cut a hole in the melon, just large enough for the monkey to insert his hand to reach the seeds inside. The monkey will stick his hand in, grab as many of the seeds as he can, then start to withdraw it. This he cannot do, since his fist is now larger than the hole. The monkey

Are You in a Trap?

People, like the ring-tailed monkey, are foolishly holding on to their beliefs.

will pull and tug, screeching and fighting the melon for hours. However, he can't get free of the trap unless he gives up the seeds, which he refuses to do. We can't but laugh at the foolish monkey! If he only would let go he would be free. But no, his love for the seeds causes him to lose his freedom.

Mankind is in a similar trap. People, like the monkey, are foolishly holding on to their beliefs, which are costing them their freedom and the knowledge of the true and living God that would lead them to the Kingdom of God.

Who is the one that has set the trap? It is none other than Satan, the God of this world.

But if our Gospel be hid, it is hid to them that are lost. In whom the god of this world hath blinded the minds of them that believe not. Lest the light of the glorious gospel of Christ, who is the image of God, should shine unto them (2 Cor. 4:3,4).

NATURAL	REPENT		SPIRITUAL
BORN IN SIN			BORN OF GOD
DEATH			LIFE

The Mystery of God Revealed

During the time that God revealed Himself to my family and me, God always directed me to those things that would be a confirmation and that eventually would confound the people of this world. The Mystery Babylon and the history concerning Christmas and Easter are good examples. I was hungry for the truth and was never just satisfied with what God had laid on my heart. I was always looking for confirmation and as the Bible says to search and you will find, I was always determined to find what I was looking for.

Without historical or other confirmation most people would think that we were just imagining things, but with proper information it would be difficult for anyone to argue over our teachings and contest them.

When God revealed to us who Adam and Eve were, it was easy to understand that they were not the first man and woman, as I had been made to believe when I was a child. I was always made to believe that the forbidden fruit was an apple and that all of mankind was cursed as a result of Eve convincing Adam to eat from the apple. It seems silly when I look back now. Believe it or not, most people still believe in this fairy tale story today.

Searching for the truth, I soon read numerous articles that revealed the approximate age of the earth to be 10 billion years or even more. In following years when

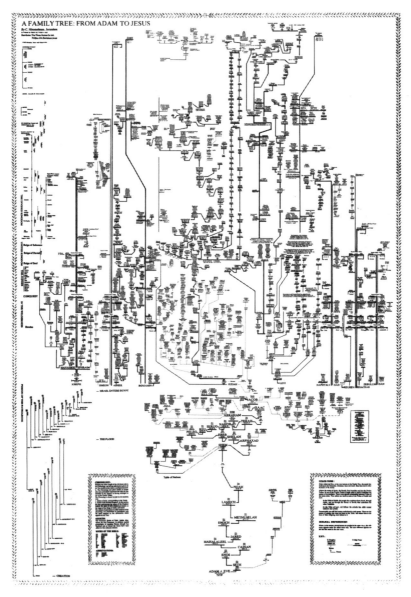

A family tree from Adam to Jesus Christ confirms the time period to be 4000 years.

THE
MISSING LINK

How did humans develop? Fossil bones found
in Ethiopia are the best clues so far.

LUCY: Lived 3.2 million years ago
■ Two-thirds complete skeleton found –
a female with long arms, short legs,
funnel-shaped chest and V-shaped jaw.
■ Scientists nicknamed her Lucy.
■ Pelvis indicates an upright but not fully
human walk.

Reconstructed
skull of a male
from Hadar

5 ft.

4

3 ft. 7 in.
tall

3

2

1

Modern woman   Lucy

Two major fossil finds

SUDAN
ERITREA   YEMEN
Red Sea
Gulf of Aden

Hadar
Site of
"Lucy"
discovery

AFRICA

Aramis
Site of *A.
ramidus*
discovery

Enlarge
d area
Addis
Ababa   DJIBOUTI

ETHIOPIA

SOMALIA

5 miles   KENYA   Indian
200 miles   Ocean

NEWLY FOUND SPECIES: Lived 4.4 million years ago
■ Fossils from 17 individuals, discovered in September. A
hominid species the scientists named *Australopithecus
ramidus* – "root of the southern apes."
■ They still lived in forests; later species ventured out onto
the plains. Bones and teeth suggest it walked upright.

I saw numerous articles regarding the discovery of human remains that were not only thousands but even millions of years old, the whole puzzle of God's creation came slowly together piece by piece.

It is common knowledge that Adam and Eve lived in an area presently called Iraq (south of Baghdad) some 4000 years before Christ and that civilizations then existed worldwide and on all continents. To prove the age of Adam and Eve, I even located a copy of a family tree in Bethlehem, Israel, detailing the offspring of Adam and Eve to the birth of Christ. And, indeed, the time period between Adam and Christ was 4000 years.

In the early days of National Geographic magazine (1904), it published a long, detailed article on the days

83

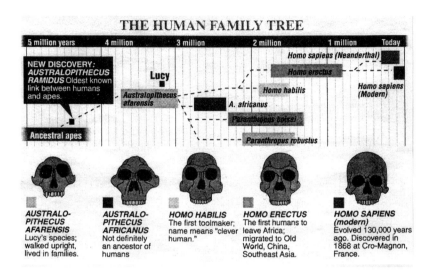

THE HUMAN FAMILY TREE

AUSTRALO-PITHECUS AFARENSIS
Lucy's species; walked upright, lived in families.

AUSTRALO-PITHECUS AFRICANUS
Not definitely an ancestor of humans

HOMO HABILIS
The first toolmaker; name means "clever human."

HOMO ERECTUS
The first humans to leave Africa; migrated to Old World, China, Southeast Asia.

HOMO SAPIENS (modern)
Evolved 130,000 years ago. Discovered in 1868 at Cro-Magnon, France.

of Adam and Eve and the civilization they lived in around 4000 BC.

When God called Adam to teach mankind about the true and living God, things did not go well for Adam and Eve, as they partook of the wicked and sinful ways of mankind.

During the days of Adam and Eve, mankind enjoyed a much shorter lifespan than the people do in today's world. Showing God's infinite power over all things, Adam lived to be 920 years old. Adam's death was the result of God's separation from Adam.

God also destroyed the offspring of Adam. The Sons of God had started to live according to the flesh and not according to God's Spirit. They had become so wicked that they married the woman of this world and for this reason God destroyed them but for Noah.

Trust me, this is not a fantasy created by me but it is all clearly recorded in the Bible in Gen 6:1-7. During the next 3000 years God would reveal Himself through numerous prophets and left us the Old Testament as proof of their attempts to teach mankind about the ways

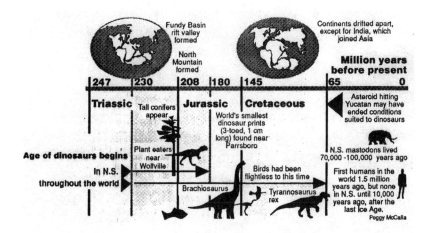

Land formation of Eastern Canada. History has proven that humanity existed throughout the world by the time Adam and Eve were chosen, approximately 4000 BC.

of the true and living God. Unfortunately, it was to no avail, as mankind preferred the spirit of darkness rather than the light. For this reason God decided to reveal Himself through Jesus Christ – but they crucified Him as an evildoer.

JOHN 3:19. AND THIS IS THE CONDEMNATION, THAT LIGHT IS COME INTO THE WORLD, AND MEN LOVED DARKNESS RATHER THAN LIGHT, BECAUSE THEIR DEEDS WERE EVIL.

The following steps can be easily followed in more detail in the Bible. They cover the seven time frames and the voice of the seven angels during which God manifested himself to fulfill his plan.

Rev 10:7 BUT IN THE DAYS OF THE VOICE OF THE SEVENTH ANGEL, WHEN HE SHALL BEGIN TO SOUND, **THE MYSTERY OF GOD** SHOULD BE FIN-

ISHED, AS HE HATH DECLARED TO HIS SERVANTS
THE PROPHETS.

God's creation.

Everything was good.

There was no evil.

Mankind, without union with God, was not
a living soul (Gen 2:5).

The earth is claimed to be approximately
10 billion years old.

Rebellion against God by Lucifer and a third of the
angels (cast out to the earth).

God's mystery plan to set up His everlasting Kingdom with mankind and to defeat Satan.

GOD'S UNION WITH MANKIND

- God formed Adam (first Son of God) to teach man-
  kind about God (appr. 4000 years BC).
- God made Eve to be Adam's handmaiden.
- There was no need for Adam and Eve to have chil-
  dren. This is a great mystery (Eph 5:28-32).
- Through Adam mankind was to come to the knowl-
  edge of God.
- All authority over all things was given to Adam.
- Adam and Eve were perfect and knew no evil.

GOD SEPARATED HIMSELF FROM ADAM

- Adam and Eve sinned as they partook of the ways of
  mankind (ate from the forbidden fruit).
- At this point they still knew God even though their
  bodies (flesh) had become corrupt since sin entered
  in.
- At this point they knew the difference between good
  (God) and evil (Satan).

- At this point God still provided for Adam and Eve.
- Eve would have to bear children like mankind.
- Adam would have to labor like mankind.
- Sin had entered in and for this reason God separated Himself from Adam and Eve.

SATAN'S KINGDOM

- In order to keep the Tree of Life, God separated Himself from mankind, otherwise mankind would have totally corrupted it.
- As sin entered in through one man (Adam), all of mankind came to live under the power of the devil (sin).
- The Sons of God started to live according to the flesh and not according to God's Spirit. They had become so wicked as they married the woman of this world that God destroyed them but for Noah (Gen. 6:1-7).

GOD'S EXAMPLE FOR MANKIND TO FOLLOW

- God came into the world in the name of Jesus Christ to destroy the works of the devil (Satan). He became flesh (sin) for us.
- Christ became the example for man to follow.
- Only way back to God (Father) is through Christ.
- First followers (chosen ones) were the twelve apostles of Christ.
- Through religious doctrines Satan transformed himself into an angel of light and claimed himself to be Christ. His servants claim to be apostles of Christ.
- Satan deceiving this whole world (Rev 12:9).
- Man reads the scriptures but cannot understand the word of God.
- Man given the choice to Repent and to turn from

darkness to light and from the power of Satan unto God (Acts 26:18).

CHOICE FOR MANKIND TO REPENT AND TO TURN FROM DARKNESS TO LIGHT AND FROM THE POWER OF SATAN UNTO GOD (ACTS 26:18)

- Unglorified state of man.
- Knowledge of God (Christ) revealed to those whom God chooses.
- Those who overcome the spirit of this world (Repent) become born of God and the sons of God, as the Father adopts those that belong to Him.
- Those that are born of God live in the world but are not of the world.
- In reading the word of God they understand every word.
- Those born of God know the difference between good (God) and evil (Satan).
- God takes care of all those that belong to Him. The believers live by faith and rely on God alone, as He has power over all things including the flesh.
- The believers have sin (live in the flesh), but do not sin.
- God chooses His servants. Many are called but few are chosen.
- Those that are born of God cannot be received by this world. For this reason Christ was crucified.

THE RETURN OF CHRIST

- All those that belong to Christ will rise with Him, dressed with a new body (first resurrection).
- Back to perfection (original Adam).

- Those that have risen with Christ will neither marry, nor are given in marriage, neither can they die any more (Luke 20:35-36).
- Christ along with his servants will teach all those that are left in this world about the ways of God (Adam's original purpose).
- Christ's 1,000-year reign.
- Christ's authority over all things.
- Final judgement.

GOD'S PLAN COMPLETED

- New Heaven and new Earth being created.
- God's everlasting Kingdom.
- God's plan fulfilled and complete.

1 John 4:4-6

Ye are of God, little children, and have overcome them: because greater is he that is in you, than he that is in the world. They are of the world: therefore speak they of the world, and the world heareth them. We are of God: he that knoweth God heareth us; he that is not of God heareth not us. Hereby know we the spirit of truth, and the spirit of error.

NATURAL	REPENT		SPIRITUAL
BORN IN SIN			BORN OF GOD
DEATH			LIFE

Fellow Servants

In 1988 I found myself working for one of the largest chemical companies in the world. It had a large agricultural division but I worked for the smaller forestry division as a forestry specialist. I traveled extensively throughout Eastern Canada and Dianne accompanied me on many of my trips.

The company did well and we found ourselves travelling to Scottsdale, Arizona; Vancouver; Toronto; Quebec City; etc.; for conferences or meetings. I enjoyed my work and the people I dealt with. As part of my job I spent a lot of my time in the outdoors and was close to nature.

In the spring of 1991, I traveled to St. Louis, Missouri, to attend a two-week training program. While there, I met another Canadian who attended the course. During the two weeks we did not see a lot of each other and it was not till we left and were awaiting our flight at the airport, that we started to communicate.

I learned then that he had grown up on a farm in Western Canada. We were both leaving for Winnipeg, Manitoba, where we had to attend the national meeting. We had a long wait for our flight and, sitting in the airport lounge, we started discussing different issues and it was not long before we brought God into the equation. Without any strife or division, it seemed that he understood everything God had revealed to me about Himself.

Since the conference did not start until the following Monday we had the whole weekend to ourselves and we continued our dialogue about the many things we had in common. Like myself in 1984, he realized that for many years he had been blind but now he could see.

After we went our respective ways we continued to share our common beliefs. I believe that God placed us 4000 km apart, so we could not be accused of influencing each other.

As employees of the company (which employed 55,000 people worldwide) we received a copy of a book that had been written by the company's President and CEO. His ambition was to build the company into one of the largest and most successful companies in the world. They had become one of the leaders in biochemical engineering and had already produced an artificial sweetener, which had become one of their big profit generators. They had produced an artificial fattener and were also starting to market an artificial cow hormone that could significantly increase the milk production of a cow.

With all humility and boldness I wrote to the president and gave him my thoughts on his book and also about some of the things God had taught me. Basically, I told him he was on the wrong track.

In the fall of that year I was nominated for the master sales award but things took a different turn a few months later.

I was given 12 hours' notice to attend a meeting in a downtown hotel in Halifax. Here four people confronted me with a letter of severance, which I had to accept and sign. The reason given was downsizing.

As soon as I arrived home, I forwarded a letter to the president, requesting to know if my earlier correspondence had anything to do with my severance. As expected,

I never received a reply but (as another manifestation of God) the little guy resigned six months later.

Before his resignation I did receive a call from Mr. Don Thomander. At the time he was the head of the Criminal Investigation Division for the RCMP in Halifax, Nova Scotia. Apparently, the company was quite upset that I had forwarded my personal testimony, outlining my beliefs in the true and living God, to many people in the company.

Mr. Thomander threatened me with further action if I did not stop this practice, only to receive a firm letter from me informing him that, under the Canadian Charter of Freedom and Rights, I was doing nothing wrong. That was the last I ever heard from him.

During this time, I had also gone out distributing copies of my testimony and placing them on windshields of cars. A few months later I was told that the City of Halifax had passed a bylaw making the placing of advertising on car windshields illegal.

I know that the company had made the connection between my friend and myself and as a consequence the company released him from his duties as well. Turning to God can be a frightening experience. The first years into our faith were very difficult as our faith was severely tested on many occasions. Our friends discovered this as well. Their biggest test came when their first baby died during birth and I cannot even imagine what they must have gone through. The thought of the two of them carrying a little box with their baby into the cemetery broke our hearts. But they persevered and, over the years, they grew in faith and, thanks be to God, they are now blessed with a total of six beautiful children.

As fellow servants in Christ they have been a blessing to us throughout our journey. They are the first ones we turn to when God allows us to suffer. Many times we have called each other and asked each other to pray for one another when we felt the rope slipping through our hands. And each time we did, God listened.

1 John 5:4

For whatsoever is born of God overcometh the world: and this is the victory that overcometh the world, even our faith.

NATURAL	REPENT		SPIRITUAL
BORN IN SIN			BORN OF GOD
DEATH			LIFE

The Virgin Birth and the Appearances of Mary

The fact that Mary was a virgin when she conceived and became pregnant is another one of those mysteries that has been covered in the past but is now being revealed. Every human is born through the sinful seed of his/her father and for this reason everyone that becomes Born of God needs to repent (change) from the spirit of darkness to the spirit of light and from the power of Satan unto God (Acts 26:18). Jesus Christ (God in the flesh) came into this world, not through the sinful seed of Joseph but because Mary was chosen to bring Jesus Christ into the world by the power of God. Since the Spirit of His Father dwelt in Him intrinsically there was no need for Him to repent, as mankind must. He could have ruled the world as He had power and authority over all things, but He came simply into this world as an example for others to follow. It was not the time yet to set up His Kingdom and it would allow an opportunity for others to be saved.

If his mother Mary died in Christ (only God is the judge), she went to sleep as is the case with all other believers. All those that belong to Christ will rise with Him dressed with a new body (first resurrection), when Christ returns.

As explained earlier in the Mystery Babylon, the worshipping of saints and the Virgin Mary was derived from many of the Babylonian rites and practices. Anyone with a little knowledge of God and the Bible would know that every imagined appearance of Mary in places like Lourdes, Fatima or elsewhere is a lie. This was made possible by the high-minded thinking of children, in most cases stirred up by the parents and the church. It is simply the imagination of the human mind. It is very similar to the deception that, as the youngest boy of a family of nine, I should become a priest and attend the seminary. It was only the imagination, the high-minded thinking of my parents and the many years of conditioning of their minds (through religion) that instilled that belief.

The claim that people have been healed from their illnesses or diseases while visiting those so-called holy shrines in Lourdes and Fatima is a false claim and is an abomination in the eyes of God. People do not have to go to Lourdes or Fatima to leave their crutches. They can simply put them away at home and it would have the same result. The human mind is a powerful weapon and it is what the devil uses to keep every man, woman and child in his power and separated from God. This is why the Bible teaches us to turn ourselves daily to the true and living God for repentance and the renewing and transformation of our minds.

Another absurdity is the proclamation by Pope Pius IX, in 1845 AD, that Mary was born without original sin. Only Jesus Christ was conceived by the power of God. Mary, like all of mankind, was conceived through the sinful seed of her natural father and by nature she was born in sin.

Many people still follow a custom of the burning of candles in front of statues and/or different images of the Lady of Fatima, Lourdes, Guadalupe or others.

The main purpose for following this tradition is in the hope that people can win favors for the dead or even for themselves. This also is an abomination as Jesus Christ is the only intercessor. The only way people can get to know Him is through repentance and to turn from darkness to light and from the power of Satan unto God (Acts 26:18). Through repentance their eyes will be opened and they will learn that through the traditions of mankind Satan has transformed himself into an angel of light and has people believe that he is God.

In most European countries there are literally dozens of cities and towns that have so-called Holy Shrines. Most countries have their own traditions and customs and Mexico is no exception. There, on December 12, they celebrate the feast of the "Lady of Guadalupe", also named the Virgin. The nation's devotion to the Virgin, also known as the "Queen of Mexico", has made the Basilica of Guadalupe the most visited so-called holy site after Mecca, receiving 13 to 14 million pilgrims annually.

But in Mexico, the Virgin is much more than a beloved patron saint. For many Mexicans she is also an important part of their identity, the symbolic "crux of the mestizo nation" that emerged from the Spanish conquest. According to legend, the dark-skinned Virgin (they even changed the color to their own liking), appeared to Juan Diego in 1531 and asked him, speaking in the Nahuatl language, to build a temple for her over a site where Aztecs worshipped Tonantzin, one of their deities. In 2002, Pope John Paul canonized Juan Diego, making him the first Indian saint of the Americas (see Chapter 16 of this book on Sainthood by the Pope).

In Mexico alone there are 17 cities and towns that make a reference to the name of Guadalupe. Most Mexicans celebrate the Guadalupe feast day of December 12 in local processions and church festivities. In fact, there are processions most evenings leading up to the actual feast day. Some people will even go for miles on their knees carrying a statue and image of the "Lady" to the altar of their local churches, in order to find favor with her.

If you have ever traveled by bus through Mexico, you would have noticed that most buses display a crucifix of Jesus Christ or a picture of the Virgin. Bus drivers in Mexico are the worst and often described as the most radical drivers in the world (maniacs is a better word to describe some of them), but despite all this, the display of religious relics is supposed to protect them somehow. Similar beliefs can likewise be found in other countries throughout the world.

Most Mexicans also believe the Lady of Guadalupe to be an intercessor to God. Now we not only have the Virgin Mary but the Lady of Guadalupe, the Lady of Fatima (my mother's favorite), the Lady of Lourdes and I am sure there are many others that I have not even heard of. It seems that these days just about every country has its own Queen of Heaven. The tradition of worshipping the Queen of Heaven, by the way, was observed by many cultures during Old Testament times and before the Virgin Mary was ever heard of.

Throughout the history of mankind, nothing has been more convincing than the traditions and doctrines people have grown up with and have been conditioned by, especially children. The tradition of Santa Claus is a good example. Going to church falls into the same category.

Most of our attitudes and ideas are formed before we reach adulthood. Religious traditions and doctrines become so deep-rooted by then that nobody is even allowed to challenge the history or values of such traditions. Traditions and customs are for most people a form of security blanket, which nobody is allowed to disturb.

Religion has always been the most powerful stronghold of Satan through which he has exercised his force and power throughout this world (remember the Inquisition). Mankind attempts to fulfill its psychological and emotional needs through it. Throughout the history of mankind, religion has had the power to overthrow whole governments and has created more world conflicts than any other issue. It is continuing to do so today in all corners of the world.

All of the appearances by the Virgin Mary and the view that she is an intercessor to God is superstitious absurdity. As mentioned earlier, there is only one way to the Father and that is through the Lord Jesus Christ. The Bible makes this very clear. The devil has tried to convince mankind of every imaginable way but there is still only the one way.

Col 2:8

Beware lest any man spoil you through philosophy and vain deceit, after the tradition of men, after the rudiments of the world, and not after Christ.

NATURAL	REPENT		SPIRITUAL
BORN IN SIN			BORN OF GOD
DEATH			LIFE

Sainthood by the Pope

One of the greatest abominations is the declaration of saints by the pope. First of all, to declare himself a descendant of Peter is a lie and to declare that Peter was a pope is an abomination and a fabrication of the truth.

Studying the early church will reveal that it took hundreds of years for the papacy to be established and it was Leo, who was the bishop of Rome from 390 to 461 AD, who first made the claim that Peter had been the first pope (see chapter 9 on Popes). The claim that the chair of Peter is still used by the pope today is laughable.

There are only a few times that the church makes reference to Satan. The most significant time is during Baptism, when it claims the newly-born baby to be free from the powers of Satan for the rest of his/her life. Little does the church know that the powers of Satan (spirit of darkness) will control everyone the rest of their lives and unless they repent they will die under the power of that same spirit (the power of sin).

There was another important time in the church that the word Satan was used. Pope Leo XIII, in 1884, declared in an official bulletin from the Vatican that the human race was divided into two opposing parties. One was the Kingdom of God on earth and the other the Kingdom of Satan. Even though the Bible is very clear that Christ will return to set up His Kingdom, church rulers have no knowledge that this present world is Satan's Kingdom and that they are the servants thereof.

So, what about the doctrine of saints? Pope John Paul II accelerated the whole process of making new saints: the more the merrier. In order to speed it up, he even changed the rules. Why not? He could do whatever he wanted, as absolute power was arranged for him by the doctrine of papal infallibility. This was agreed by only a marginal vote during the First Vatican Council in 1869.

Under John Paul II, in order to qualify for sainthood, a person only needed to perform one miracle (it had been two). The Bible teaches us that the devil also would perform miracles in the latter days. Another requirement was a certificate of spiritual cleanness. That is it, you are now officially a saint by Vatican standards. I wonder how anyone would obtain a written declaration of spiritual cleanness. I have never heard of a mail service between God and the Vatican. The whole thing is laughable, if you sit back and think about it.

So, how does one become a true Saint? Every believer in God's eyes, and as confirmed by the Bible, is a Saint. It is interesting to note that the word "saint", which in the Catholic tradition has been reserved for a few selected individuals, was in the Early Church the common word applied to all believers in Christ (Rom 1:7, 1 Cor 1:2, Eph 1:18). All those, declared Saints by the Pope died in their sins, as will the Pope himself, unless of course he repents.

Satan is a master deceiver and he knows how to pick his people. Consider the recent pope, John Paul II, how revered he was by his followers. He was hardly able to speak or stand, but still thousands flocked to the Vatican to see him.

Or consider Mother Theresa who worked with the sick. What is wrong with the millions of nurses who care for the sick every day? I have two sisters who cared for the sick their whole lives. How come they are not saints?

The world needs its heroes. While there is one King who died for all and who was crucified, the people of this world have their heroes whom they call "king". They called Elvis the king. They called Richard Petty the king of auto racing. They called Pele the king of soccer, and now they call Wayne Gretzky the king of hockey. How about religious heroes like the Pope, Mother Theresa, the local Bishop or priest, and so on? And don't let us forget the political heroes of this world, and heroes and idols in the world of entertainment and sports. I am sure there are many more but your worshipping of idols and heroes will be to no avail.

Despite John Paul II's popularity, he could not even keep his bishops or priests from abusing thousands of young boys, abuse that is continuing today. All because he did not know what spirit he served.

Throughout the church calendar almost every day has been set aside to celebrate the feast of a particular saint. Most of them have been borrowed from ancient paganism as are Halloween and Valentine's Day.

Halloween

Ghosts, ghouls, goblins, trolls, demons, poltergeists, black cats, witches, broomsticks, skeletons and jack-o-lanterns. What is it all about? Many observe Halloween but don't know why.

Halloween began long before "Christianity" during the days of the pagan priesthood of the Druids of Ireland, with the belief that this is the one night in the year that ghosts and witches are most likely to wander about. The earliest Halloween celebrations were held in honor of "Samhain" or Satan, the lord of the dead. It was also an ancient Roman celebration held as a festival in honor of the ancient Roman goddess, Pomona. When people dress up as demons, witches, goblins and skeletons, they are mimicking Satan, the devil, and demons. They are acting out the capricious frolicking of the ancient pagans who masqueraded as evil spirits, or who built fires, left gifts and offerings to placate the impish, macabre spirits, as well as "Samhain" the lord of the dead. On October 31, Halloween is observed as the Eve of All Hallows or Hallowmas. It is still regarded by many today as a church festival commemorating the evening before All Saints Day, which is on November 1.

How many customs have been borrowed from ancient paganism? For openers there is Christmas, Easter, New Years and Halloween. A few moments research in some of the higher level encyclopedias will prove that Halloween is also a pagan celebration.

Valentine

Valentine's Day has been traced to the old Roman festival of Lupercalia, which occurred in February.

During the weeklong feast honoring the God Lupercus, young men drew lots for the names of their prospective sweethearts and, thus, partners were matched for the coming year. When the early so-called Christian fathers, sought to eliminate pagan customs, they substituted February 14 for the Lupercalian festival, they day on which they said Saint Valentine was murdered.

The Roman Church bestowed so-called sainthood upon several Valentines. The most prominent are two individuals whose feasts are both celebrated on February 14, one a priest who died at Rome, and the other the

Bishop of Terni (Interamna). Although very little is known for certain about either, they seem to have died on the same day (c. 270) and to have been buried at different places along the Flaminian Way. A few moments of research will prove that Valentine's Day is strictly a pagan celebration.

1 Cor 2:12-15

Now we have received, not the spirit of the world, but the spirit which is of God; that we might know the things that are freely given to us of God. Which things also we speak, not in the words which man's wisdom teacheth, but which the Holy Ghost teacheth; comparing spiritual things with spiritual. But the natural man receiveth not the things of the Spirit of God: for they are foolishness unto him: neither can he know them, because they are spiritually discerned. But he that is spiritual judgeth all things, yet he himself is judged of no man.

NATURAL	REPENT	SPIRITUAL
BORN IN SIN		BORN OF GOD
DEATH		LIFE

The Abomination of Desolation

The abomination of desolation referred to in the Bible signifies a particular false sacrifice. Of all the abominations that modern religions have introduced, the one that stands out as the abomination of desolation, as spoken of by Daniel the prophet and also spoken of in the Book of Revelation, is the Consecration instituted by the Roman Catholic Church. Let us go back and retrace the mystery of this abomination (see The Mystery Babylon).

The Mass as a celebration was adopted in 349 AD and many other celebrations were adopted around the same time, for example, the veneration of angels and so-called dead saints, the worship of Mary, etc. Gradually, the Mass was developed as a sacrifice of Christ on the cross, and became obligatory in the eleventh century. The dogma of transubstantiation was decreed by Pope Innocent III in 1215 AD. Please remember it is a man-made doctrine instituted more than a thousand years after Jesus Christ died. According to this doctrine, the priest miraculously changes wine into the blood of Christ and the communion wafer into the actual body of Christ, and these he then proceeds to drink and eat before the congregation.

Of all of the doctrines, traditions and customs in the world religions practiced today, this is the one most appalling to God. One cannot even describe how absurd and superstitious this celebration is, especially if one even considers the words that are being used.

When I was a young boy and being prepared for first communion, we were informed that the communion wafer could not be touched by your teeth or by your finger. As a young boy I used to break out into a sweat, when it used to stick to the roof of my mouth and I didn't know what to do.

Another abomination and absurdity is the "sacrament" of confession. Also, a man-made doctrine instituted by Pope Innocent III in 1215 AD. Sin is not an act as they have made you believe, but is the fruit of the natural spirit of mankind. It is what continues to separate mankind from God.

People should know, if only by reading the history of the Inquisition, that the Roman Catholic Church had nothing to do with the teachings of Christ. The objective of the Inquisition was to gain world dominance by eliminating those that did not follow the doctrines of Rome. Only Satan would use force. God allows people to make a personal choice to repent and to turn from darkness to light and from the power of Satan unto God (Acts 26:18). Another item that does not often come up for discussion is the subject of the creation of large Catholic families as a means to increase the numbers of the Catholic church.

My mother has only recently opened this discussion since the death of my father a number of years ago. We always knew that there was a lot of pressure by the church to have large families but my mother told us that, if she was not pregnant within a year of the birth of a child, the local priest would visit. In a subtle way he would then ask when the next child was going to be born and if there was a problem.

It was also customary to give a donation to a visiting priest. In those days my dad was trying to raise a family from three acres of land and most of the time it was difficult to keep the family fed, especially during the years of WW II. Regardless of those circumstances, the visiting priest, after leaving my mom and dad with his subtle message about having more children, would not go away empty-handed.

When my mother talks about those times now, she looks back with disgust at how they used the power of the church to manipulate the people. Still, she cannot let go of the traditions she grew up with and continues to remain in bondage to the doctrines of the church as she, unfortunately, does not want to acknowledge what spirit she is of, as does the rest of my natural family. Besides the nine children my mom had, she also told one of my sisters a few years ago that she also had two miscarriages. Most of my brothers and sisters are a year apart and where there was a two-year spread, was the time my mother had a miscarriage.

Another abomination is the claim by the pope that he is the vicar or direct representative of Christ. In the last 30 years, God has manifested Himself in many ways and clearly shown mankind what spirit they are of, through the many sex-abuse cases that have surfaced. Their own man-made doctrine of celibacy, which was decreed by Pope Hildebrand Gregory VII in 1079 AD, has also become a curse to them. Christ never imposed such rules and neither did the apostles. Peter was married and Paul states that bishops were to have one wife and could have children (1 Tim. 3:5,12; Matt. 8:14,15).

There has been a lot of debate during the last decade on the issue of abortion and birth control and what the position of the church is on that subject. Their discussion is all to no avail. The very nature of mankind is enmity with God and the very nature of mankind is sinful.

Sin is not an act as they try to make you believe. The very workings of mankind is sinful and sin is the fruit of every man, woman and child.

For this reason they are called to repentance.

The claim by the papacy that it serves the Holy Office is a lie as it is not holy at all. It is a man-made office with no connection to God but to the spirit of this world and controlled by Satan (spirit of darkness).

All other abominations I have already discussed in this book.

NATURAL	REPENT	SPIRITUAL
BORN IN SIN		BORN OF GOD
DEATH		LIFE

Spiritual Blindness

The history of mankind is written in human blood because it refuses to listen and accept the teachings of God. For this reason mankind remains spiritually blind and separated from God. The life, suffering and the blood of Jesus Christ took care of every problem in this world but mankind prefers to worship its idols and images rather than the true and living God.

Billy Graham doesn't teach the Gospel of Jesus Christ. Ever notice how many people attend his crusades? In 1988 we wrote him only to receive a reply from his Executive Assistant to inform us that Billy Graham was born again. The following was our reply back to him.

January 21, 1989
Billy Graham Evangelistic Association
1300 Harmon Place
Minneapolis, Minnesota 55403 USA

Attention: Victor B. Nelson

Dear Sir:
The purpose of my earlier writing was with the hope that you would be able to acknowledge that you are a sinner and under the power thereof (power of Satan). However, since by nature you say you see, your sin will remain and you will continue

to be spiritually blind (John 9:41).

Because you did not believe in the Lord Jesus Christ in the things I wrote and never did RE-PENT your eyes have been blinded and your heart has been hardened, that you should not see with your eyes, nor understand with your heart. Nor will you be converted for you do not believe in the Lord Jesus Christ but in a false image of God, a false Christ and a lie (2 Thess 2:11).

By nature you decided at some point in time in your life to become a minister, you were never chosen by God as you had never turned to Him. By nature you started to use the Word of God and stole the name of my Lord and Savior as you transformed yourself into an apostle of Christ. It is for this reason this world loves you while God's servants are not of this world (born again) but God chose them out of this world, therefore, the world hates them (John 15:19).

You speak according to man's wisdom and according to the wisdom of this world (1 Cor 2: 4-8). It is for this reason you call yourself doctor and claim yourself to be wise in the wisdom of this world (1 Cor 1:20).

But I certify you, that the Gospel which I preach is not after man, for I never received it of man (as you did) neither was I taught it, but by revelation of Jesus Christ (Gal 1: 11,12).

Even though you cannot understand the things that I am telling you, for the natural man receiveth not the things of the Spirit of God (1 Cor 2:14). You must first REPENT (change spirits) in order to be able to receive what is from God. Be assured, that God will bring to naught the workings of evil, Billy Graham ministries included, by His servants the prophets.

Concerning the 22,000 people whom you believe accepted the Lord Jesus Christ on the last Billy Graham crusades let me just say: how can they accept Christ from one who preaches a false Christ (Rom 10: 14,15)?

There shall arise false Christs, and false prophets (Matt 24:24) and if it were possible **even the very elect** would be deceived. Woe unto you, scribes and pharisees (religious folks, doctors and theologians), for you compass sea and land to make one proselyte (convert), and when he is made, ye make him twofold more the child of hell than yourselves (Matt 23:15).

Ye know not what manner of spirit ye are of (Luke 9:55) but you will see yourself the manifestation of the sons of God and you will know yourself that Billy Graham was never sent or chosen by God but is a servant of sin by nature, like yourself, he was born that way and never changed spirits (Repented) and was never born again.

Whatsoever is born of God overcomes the world (1 John 5:4). The reason you never overcame the spirit of this world (Satan) is because you never did turn to the true and living God that He could convert you and could transform you into His likeness.

For this purpose the Son of God was manifested that He might destroy the works of the devil (1 John 3:8).

Many deceivers are entered into the world, who confess not that Jesus Christ is come in the flesh. This is why you are different from Christ.

This is a deceiver and an antichrist. Without having ever met Mr. Graham or yourself I could list at least 100 reasons that would show you that you do not confess that Jesus Christ is come in the flesh.

It is my hope that Billy Graham gets to read my earlier letter, for even though you yourself do not believe in Jesus Christ, it is my hope that he will. You will not only be held responsible for your own sin but also for all those from whom you withhold the truth.

Jesus Christ was crucified by this world.

Matthew was martyred by this world in Ethiopia.

Mark was martyred by this world in Alexandria.

Luke was hanged by this world in Greece.

Peter was crucified by this world in Rome.

James the Great was beheaded by this world in Jerusalem.

James the Less was beaten to death by this world.

Phillip was hanged by this world in Hieropolis.

Bartholomew was flayed alive by this world.

Thomas was slain with a lance by this world at Coromandel.

Jude was killed with arrows by this world.

Simon was crucified by this world in Persia.

Andrew was crucified by this world.

Matthias was beheaded by this world.

Barnabas was stoned to death by this world.

Paul was beheaded by this world.

The above were born of God as it says in:

John 14:17 - Whom the world cannot receive

John 15:18 - If the world hate you

John 15:19 - not of the world

John 15:19 - Therefore the world hates you

John 15:20 - They will also persecute you

John 15:21 - They know not him that sent me

John 17:14 - The world hath hated them

John 17:16 - They are not of the world

Billy Graham, along with Jerry Falwell, was recently invited to the inauguration of George Bush. A $30-million-dollar splash of pageantry, color and glitter by the adulterers and spirit of this world. The reason they were invited is because they are all of the same spirit (Satan) and under the power thereof (power of darkness).

John 15:19 - If you were of the world, the world would love his own.

Luke 9:55 - Ye know not what manner of spirit ye are of.

Matt 15:14 - If the blind lead the blind, both shall fall into the ditch.

You most certainly will fall and so will the nation of the USA and all the nations of the world. Matt 23:33,34: Ye serpants, ye generation of vipers, how can you escape the damnation of hell. Wherefore, behold, I send unto you prophets and wise men, and scribes; and some of them ye shall kill and crucify; and some of them shall ye scourge in your synagogues, and persecute them from city to city.
In the love and service of my Lord and Savior Jesus Christ.
Signed: Andy G. van den Berg

Even Oprah Winfrey teaches now on spirituality; hers also has nothing to do with the Spirit of God. How about Dr. Phil, can he help you? I am afraid not.
We prophesied that Jimmy Swaggart and Jimmy and Tammy Bakker would fall. Did you know that so many people tuned into Jimmy Swaggart every Sunday that he generated $200 million annually? Even after his first fall he went back to the pulpit and once

again I prophesied that God would visit his sin. When He did, they still did not want to acknowledge that I had sent them a message of truth.

Or Ralph Rutledge, a Canadian Pentecostal minister, who had his own TV show, called the Revival Hour. I personally called him on the phone to warn him that God would bring him to an open shame. Within six months after testifying to him, I opened the local paper one evening and read that he had been accused in a sex scandal.

Please note the following two letters I wrote to Mr. Rutledge.

> August 29, 1989
> Mr. Ralph Rutledge
> Box 700, Station U
> Toronto, On M8Z 5P9
>
> Dear Sir:
> It was less than two years ago that I contacted you and introduced myself as the servant of the Lord Most High. I contacted you again in the spring of this year and as a good soldier for Christ I brought you the truth about the "One" who sent me.
>
> I informed you earlier how God would visit your sin and how you would fall. I did not come then to destroy you but to save you from the deception, which is in this world (Rev 12:9) and from the powers of darkness.
>
> I also informed you:
>
> - That you were not a servant of God.

- That you were not born of God.
- That you were not preaching the gospel of my Lord and Savior Jesus Christ.
- That you presented a false Christ.
- That you were leading the people astray.
- That you don't understand the word of God (1 Cor 2:14).
- That your prayers were all in vain.

Even though God has now brought you to an open shame, it is unlikely that you will believe in my words and the Lord Jesus Christ, but maybe you can proclaim to the nation that there is a servant of God whom they must listen to.

Therefore, before it is too late, warn your sons and tell them to stop preaching a false Christ, and also your brother-in-law David Mainse, who for 26 years has been leading the people of Canada astray through 100 Huntley Street, for what he preaches has nothing to do with Christianity. If they don't listen they will fall in like manner. Don't be foolish like J. Swaggart and go back to preaching deceit, for tragedy will be greater for him the second time around, since he went back to his own vomit. I warned him on three occasions how God would visit his sin. Look at all the people that still follow him after God brought him to an open shame. The Gospel is true when it says how people prefer darkness over light (John 1: 5; 3:19).

You yourself did not believe in him that God sent into your life, but maybe this time you will. My message, however, is still the same. Ye must repent.

You never knew God and are still separated

from Him and under the power of sin (Satan) as was your whole congregation, but you never told them. Instead, you made them believe that they were born of God and as a result they still walk in darkness according to the spirit of this world.

In the love and service of my Lord and Savior Jesus Christ. Please call if I can be of help to you.
Signed: Andy G. van den Berg
Cc: David Mainse (brother-in-law of Mr. Rutledge)

And the following letter more than two years later.

October 14, 1991
Mr. Ralph Rutledge
Box 700, Station U
Toronto, ON M8Z 5P9

Dear Sir:
After I blew the trumpet back in 1985 and warned J. Swaggart that God would visit his sin, we all heard about his disgrace in 1988.

When I wrote you and even made a personal phone call, to inform you that God would visit your sin, we all know what happened when God revealed what spirit you were of.

As a good soldier for Christ did I offer my assistance to show the true way of "REPENTANCE" and the way back to the true and living God. But you did not believe then that God sent me with His love and His message of truth (John 17:23).

After God disgraced you, I sent you a follow-up letter (see copy attached), in which I asked you not to be like Jimmy Swaggart and to go back to preaching deceit. I also wrote that tragedy would be greater for him a second time since he went back to his own vomit.

And as we have heard now that the recent news concerning J. Swaggart, it is clear that God, once again, has manifested Himself through me. But, I know, even this will not convince people that they are deceived (Rev 12:9) and that God sent me with His truth and His message of repentance.

As you have seen God's hand recently during the Senate Judiciary Committee hearings on Clarence Thomas and how God has made foolish the wisdom of the wise, including those of judges, lawyers and people with the highest authority, so will God put to test and tear apart the foundations and the wisdom of the religious authorities of this world.

Do not attempt to look for time and seasons when this all will happen, for the time of judgement is already here. You are not able to see it, as a result of your own spiritual blindness. For this very reason did I call you to Repentance and called you to turn from darkness to light and from the power of Satan unto God (Acts 26:18).

But be assured, it will happen. Even the "Mystery Babylon" (the religions of this world with the Catholic institution as the head and the mother of all harlots) will eventually fall, as described in the Book of Revelation Chapter 18, but not till all things have been fulfilled. No one knows of that hour, but my Father in Heaven. Many events are still to take place and if I told you about them you would not believe me, just as you did not believe, when I told you about your own downfall.

Prospective
priests face
psychiatric
testing

Priest faces
charges

Catholic Church a haven
for perverts, inquiry told

AIDS deaths
high for priests
— newspaper

By The Associated Press

Kansas City, Mo.

AIDS has caused the deaths of
hundreds of Roman Catholic
priests in the United States,

Priest, two other men
face sex-related charges

Six Christian Brothers
charged in Ontario

Canadian pastor
removed from TV

Bishop faces sex charges

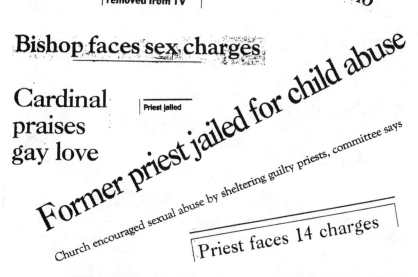

Cardinal
praises
gay love

Priest jailed

Former priest jailed for child abuse

Church encouraged sexual abuse by sheltering guilty priests, committee says

Priest faces 14 charges

Bishops knew of assaults

The headlines on this and the next page clearly reveal what spirit they are of. Nevertheless, as a result of their spiritual blindness, people continue to follow after them. The Bible refers to them as false Christs, false teachers, false prophets and blind guides.

Sex abuse by ex-minister detailed by three witnesses

Priest killed for money — Crown

Monsignor tried in bingo scam

Minister sentenced to 10 years in prison

TEMPTED BY FORBIDDEN PLEASURES, ARCHBISHOP EUGENE MARINO MEETS A SAD DOWNFALL

Bishop had many sex encounters, court was told

Minister faces charge of assaulting teen-age girl

Christian Brother gets 12 years for sexual abuse

Embryo farming a possibility—consultant

Bishop raped me, native woman says

Former archbishop sued

Priest waives preliminary on sex-related charges

Anglican church to try metro priest

As you will note I have copied numerous people who have been contacted in the past (there are many more besides these) and who also received my testimony concerning the true and living God.

But like yourself and J. Swaggart they all have resisted the Holy Ghost (Acts 7:51) and did not believe that God sent me into this world as his messenger.

As always, it is our hope that you will turn to God and I invite you, therefore, to contact us with any questions about the true and living God.

In the love and service of my Lord and Savior Jesus Christ.

Signed: Andy G. van den Berg

I can write another book about the number of times God sent me with a message of truth. That will be for another time.

During the last 20 years, papers have been full of information, detailing what spirit your priests, bishops and ministers are of. In case you have not paid attention let me refresh your memory.

Remember Jimmy Swaggart, Jimmy and Tammy Bakker and Ralph Rutledge? What spirit do you think they served?

Mail Star, Halifax, Nova Scotia, June 1989. Catholic Church a haven for perverts.

Other paper headlines: Some clergy suffer from AIDs. Minister sentenced to 10 years in prison. Minister faces charge of assaulting teen-age girl. Priest and two other men face sex-related charges.

Halifax Daily News, December 1992. Bishop raped me, native woman says.

Mail Star, December, 1992. Bishop had many sex encounters court was told.

Mail Star, December 1992. Prospective priests face psychiatric testing. The Roman Catholic Church in Nova Scotia is putting would-be priests through mandatory psychiatric examination in response to revelations of sexual abuse in the diocese of Antigonish.

Mail Star, December, 1993. Former priest jailed for child abuse.

Time, August, 1991. Catholic scandals keep spreading.

People, August, 1990. Tempted by forbidden pleasures, Archbishop Eugene Marino meets a sad downfall.

March, 1995. Cardinal praises gay love.

Austin Burke, Archbishop of Halifax, was quoted as saying that if permitted by Vatican policy, he would have no qualms about accepting the ordination of women or homosexuals by the church, if they could abide being celibate. Can it get any sillier than that? How blind are the people of this world?

Unnoticed by most people (it just happens), homosexuality has crept into society at an alarming rate. What used to be a very small minority is rapidly taking the rights away from normal relationships and wickedness abounds throughout the land, all for the satisfying of the flesh. They even try to claim now that somehow they were born with a homosexual gene.

Anyone with even a little knowledge of God would understand that homosexuality and lesbianism is a punishment from God as a result of the unbelief of the nations (Rom. 1:21-32). They even have their own churches now and do everything in the name of God, which in fact is Satan. They use every possible justification for their diabolical and unnatural lifestyle and behavior.

Four thousand years ago God tried to bring some kind of order into this world and through Moses he left mankind with the Ten Commandments as a means to show them the difference between right from wrong. Homosexuality was also an issue that Moses had been asked to deal with. God's instructions (not Moses') were to take any homosexual outside of the city walls and stone them to death. The wages of sin (human nature) are no different today and the ramifications for society far greater than mankind can imagine.

Just thirty years ago it was illegal to have a homosexual relationship. Today courts are allowing gay men and woman to marry and now they are even allowed to adopt children. Who are acting more diabolical, the people practicing homosexuality or the judges of the courts and the lawmakers of the land? Since homosexuality is practiced today by people from every walk of life (including judges and politicians), everything you are hearing of is inevitable as sin is escalating at a frightening pace. Believe me, this is just the beginning. As they say, you have seen nothing yet. It is a frightening thought to imagine what the behavior of people will be like ten years from now. The Bible is always right when it says, sin will wax worse and worse.

Let this serve as a warning to all of mankind when I declare, in the name of the true and living God, that **mankind is on the road to self-destruction, not through weapons of mass destruction but through its sinful nature and behavior.**

We have another group of people who in the last few decades have started to do things in the name of God. These are your sports and entertainment heroes. Some sport teams have their own room or chapel for worship, and pray that God will be with them. Trust me, the true and living God has nothing to do whatsoever with your success or failure.

Entertainment heroes thank God for their successes also. Award shows now take place on almost a weekly basis. The first thing they all do when they come forward to accept an award is to thank God, saying that without Him they could have never accomplished it. Sports and entertainment, just like religion, is just another way that Satan (the spirit of this world) has transformed himself into an angel of light and deceived all the people.

Today some religions have their people so confused they have their members going around saying; the Kingdom of God is already here. What kind of a God do they believe in? Would God let his people suffer from AIDS? Over 25 million are infected with the AIDS virus today.

Recently I completed studying some of the atrocities that mankind suffered as a result of individuals, during the last century starting with King Leopold of Belgium, who was responsible for the death of over 10 million people in Central Africa (the Congo). Then there was Stalin who was responsible for the murder of over 25 million people in the labor camps throughout Russia and especially northeastern Siberia. We cannot imagine what people must have experienced when they were forced to confess to crimes they never committed.

Another event that took place during the last 100 years was the First World War, the first great conflict to involve most of the civilized world. Some 65 million men were mobilized, of whom more than 8.5 million were killed or died and more than 21 million were wounded.

During the late thirties and during the Second World War Hitler systematically eliminated six million Jews. In total, more than 30 million people lost their lives during that war, at the hand of one man. Now there are some people claiming that the Holocaust never happened. Trust me, I personally know of people who have survived the torture of the concentration camps and who have seen all their family members perish before their own eyes.

In the present time there are more than 40 major conflicts going on in this world that see the destruction of human lives.

But nothing has destroyed more lives than the rule and power of the Vatican. Every Catholic should be able to understand that their religion has nothing to do with Christianity based on the atrocities of the Inquisition alone.

As during the years of Stalin, the Inquisitors used every torturous means at their disposal to get people to confess to crimes they had never committed.

But still, although history has clearly proven what spirit they serve, people cannot give up their stubbornness and, as a result, will remain separated from God and continue to live in darkness. Please understand that every religion of the modern times is somehow connected with the Roman Church. There have been thousands of other religions that have sprung up the last 2000 years and they are all offshoots from the formation of the Roman Church. Even today the Roman Catholic Church rules by domination. During the last thirty years many theologians and teachers, this including bishops, priests and nuns, with a different opinion than the Vatican, have had their licenses to teach revoked or have been demoted or placed in different positions. Some of them felt so strongly about their opinion on issues like birth control, female priests, abortion, birth control, married priests, etc., that when they were asked to retract their writings, teachings or essays, they resigned.

Truly, do you still think this is a church governed by God?

In the Body of Christ (the true church) there is absolutely no division. The wisdom and knowledge of the true and living God and the Lord Jesus Christ has always been the same.

The spiritual blindness of mankind is caused by its natural spirit, which is referred to as the devil. The only solution, as explained throughout this book, is for mankind to **REPENT**, to turn from darkness to light and from the power of Satan unto God (Acts 26:18).

NATURAL	REPENT	SPIRITUAL
BORN IN SIN		BORN OF GOD
DEATH		LIFE

Soldiers for Christ

After God revealed Himself to us, we hungered to tell people about the true and living God. For many years there was only one request during our daily prayers, that God would grant us the desires of our heart. We were still mere babes in our faith and knew very little then about the forces and principalities we would be facing when we tried to reach out to the people around us. We soon learned however that people were getting more than just upset about our message.

Like Christ (John 7:5), nobody in our own families believed or wanted to hear what we had to say and share with them. For a number of years we reached out by placing advertisements in papers in different communities and the only response we received was from people who wanted to share their opinion.

Most people in the religious circles today think that by nature they are Born of God and they truly believe that they are sons and daughters of God. The devil must have known that God was preparing people to share the truth with this world once again, as never before have so many people used the term "born again". It has only been during the last 30 years that the devil has freely started to use this expression publicly. When you travel to the southern United States, almost everybody thinks that they are Born of God and this movement is spreading rapidly through every religious denomination. While

NATURAL	REPENT		SPIRITUAL
BORN IN SIN	To repent means to change spirits. Eze 11:19,20; 18:30,31; 36:26,27; Matt 9:16,17; John 12:24; Acts 26:18; 2 Cor 5:17; Eph 4:23,24; Col 3:10.		**BORN OF GOD**
DEATH			LIFE

DO YOU BELIEVE

— That those that are mentally ill, handicapped, deaf or blind have an unclean spirit (devil), and that faith in God would make them whole (Matt 9:6,29,32; 12:22; Mark 7:35; Luke 8:48; 17:19).

— That if you believed and had faith in the living God, you would never have to see another doctor, or take medication (Deut 7:15).

— That if you are in bondage to any man made religion (listed under churches in the yellow pages), you believe in a lie and have been deceived worse, and are in greater bondage than the sick or the handicapped (Matt 15:9; John 8:33,34; Rom 8:15,21; Gal 4:3; 5:1; 2 Thess 2:11; Hebr 2:15).

— That Satan (spirit of darkness which by nature all men have been born with) has transformed himself into an angel of light (2 Cor 1:13,14) and if it were possible even the very elect would be deceived (Matt 24:22-24; Rev 12:9).

— That the TRUE CHURCH of the believers in Jesus Christ can not be received by this present world and that so called world evangelization is a deception at the highest level (John 1:5,10; 8:23; 14:17,22; 15:19,20; 17:9,14,16,25; 18:36; Rom 8:7; 1 Cor 1:20; 2:4-8; 12-14; 1 Thess 3:3; 2 Tim 3:12; Jas 4:4; 1 John 2:15; 3:1; 5:4,19; 2 John 7).

If you are confused and would like to hear the truth and be set free from the spirit of this world (sin), then join us at:

Keddy's Halifax Hotel — Atlantic Room
20 St. Margarets Bay Rd.,
Halifax, N.S.
Date: Sunday, May 8. Time: 8:00 p.m.
We will answer any questions you may have.

Advertisement in our paper dated May 7, 1988.

NATURAL	REPENT		SPIRITUAL
BORN IN SIN	Acts 26:18. To open their eyes, and to turn them from darkness to light, and from the power of Satan unto God.		**BORN OF GOD**
DEATH			LIFE

— When God entrusted the apostle Paul, and all His other servants, with the above message, why was it that they were hated, persecuted, imprisoned, beaten, called evildoers and eventually murdered for their faith by the people of this world even as their Lord Jesus Christ Himself was?

— Was it because the Gospel they preached condemned and judged every sinful man (John 16:8:9: 1 Cor 2:15)?

— Was it because they preached the Gospel in truth and not after man's wisdom (1 Cor 2:4-7: Gal 1:11,12)?

— Was it because they were ordained by God (Jer 1:5; Mark 3:14; John 15:16) and were able to love as He loved and lay down their lives for their friends as He did (John 15:9,10,13)?

— Are your popes, bishops, priests, deacons, pastors, ministers etc. chosen by God or were they ordained by men (Gal 1:1) and do they preach things you like to hear (Isa 30:9,10), after man's wisdom (Matt 15:9; 1 Tim 4:1), who spoil you through philosophy and vain deceit, after the tradition of men and the rudiments of the world, and not after Christ (Col 2:8; 2 John 7)?

— Are you hearing the Gospel in truth or are you being deceived by servants of sin, blind guides, deceitful workers, false apostles or workers of iniquity (Matt 7:23; 23:16; John 8:34; Cor 11:13)?

During the meeting of May 8 the mystery of the Gospel was explained in the same way as God has declared to His servants the prophets (Rev 10:7). Those that were present were blessed with the true Gospel. Please do join us. There will be no soliciting for funds for the gift of eternal life was freely given to us and freely do we give it to all those that believe (Matt 6:26; 10:8).

Keddy's Halifax Hotel - Atlantic Room
20 St. Margaret's Bay Rd.
Halifax, N.S.
Date: Sunday, June 5. Time: 8:00 p.m.

We will answer any questions you may have. If you are unable to attend our meeting tomorrow, the next meeting will be on June 26th at the same time and at the same place.

Advertisement in our paper dated June 4, 1988.

NATURAL	REPENT	SPIRTUAL
BORN IN SIN	Luke 15:10. There is joy in the presence of the angels of God over one sinner that repents.	**BORN OF GOD**
DEATH		LIFE

What does it mean to repent (Ezek. 14:6; 36:26, 27; Mark 6:12), to overcome the world (1 John 5:4), to be converted (Acts 3:19) and to be transformed (Rom. 12:2) into the likeness of His Son (John 17:11,22; Phil. 3:21; 2 Peter 1:4; 1 John 3:2; 4:17)?

To answer the above and any other questions you may have we will gather at:

Keddy's Motor Inn - Wentworth Room
437 Prince St.
TRURO, N.S.
Date: Sunday, Oct. 30th. Time: 7:00 p.m.

There will be no soliciting for funds for the gift of life and the knowledge to the mystery of the Kingdom (Mark 4:11) was freely given to us and freely do we give to all those that want to believe in the Gospel of our Lord and Saviour Jesus Christ (Matt. 6:26; 10:8).

For the time and place when we will visit your community in the Maritimes please watch for announcements in your local newspaper or write to us at:

(Mailing address removed for this book)

Advertisement in our paper dated October 22, 1988.

NATURAL	REPENT	SPIRTUAL
BORN IN SIN	Luke 5:10. There is joy in the presence of the angels of God over one sinner that repents.	**BORN OF GOD**
DEATH		LIFE

The religious folks say that people like Dr. Morgentaler and Allan Legere are sinners and some even say that they will die in their sins, for the wages of sin are death (Rom 6:23)

GOD SAYS

EXCEPT YE REPENT, YE SHALL ALL LIKEWISE PERISH (LUKE 13:3,5)

If you would like to know what it means to live in sin and under the power of the devil (1 John 3:8) and would like to receive your messages of REPENTANCE then please call us at ___ or write us at:

Telephone number and mailing address
removed for this book.

There will be no soliciting for funds for the gift of LIFE is a free gift to all those that believe in the truth (Matt 6:26; 10:8)

BEHOLD, I STAND AT THE DOOR AND KNOCK (REV 3:20)

66606L23

Advertisement in our paper dated December 23, 1989.

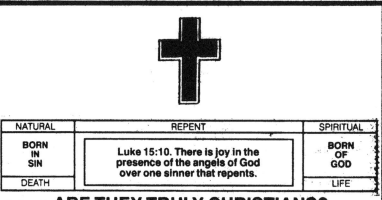

NATURAL	REPENT	SPIRITUAL
BORN IN SIN	Luke 15:10. There is joy in the presence of the angels of God over one sinner that repents.	**BORN OF GOD**
DEATH		LIFE

ARE THEY TRULY CHRISTIANS?

- Approx. 1800 years ago they called themselves: Gnostics, Montanists, Novationists, Docetists, Ebionites, Stoicists, Platonists, Pythagorean ists and Monarchians.

- Today, they call themselves Roman Catholics, Anglicans, Lutherans, Pentecostals, Seventh Day Adventists, Jehovah's Witnesses, Mennon ites, Baptists, Mormons, etc., etc.

- Are the above members of the church that was founded by the Lord Jesus Christ and the early apostles, or do they follow after a man made image of a false God in which, there is no salvation?

- Are you hearing the Gospel in truth or are you being deceived by ser vants of sin, blind guides, deceitful workers, false apostles or workers of iniquity (Matt 7:23; 23:16; John 8:34; Cor 11:13)?

- As you are witnesses now of the degradation of society and the de struction of the works of man, we encourage you to turn to the true and living God and the true Gospel as it was preached by Christ and the apostles. "For I certify you that the Gospel which was preached of me is not after man, for I neither received it of man, neither was I taught it, but by the revelation of Jesus Christ" (Gal. 1:11, 12).

Please write us if you would like to share in spiritual truth about the true and living God.

(Mailing address removed for this book)

There will be absolutely no soliciting for funds for the gift of LIFE was freely given and freely do we give to all that believe (Matt 6:26; 10:8). 24569128

Advertisement in our paper dated December 28, 1991.

NATURAL	REPENT	SPIRITUAL
BORN IN SIN	**Luke 15:10. There is joy in the presence of the angels of God over one sinner that repents.**	**BORN OF GOD**
DEATH		LIFE

HOW CAN A PERSON KNOW...

- If you serve the true and living God or a man made image of a false God (1 Chr. 5:25; Mark 12:32)?
- If you follow after the Lord Jesus Christ or a false Christ (Matt. 24:4,5,24)?
- If you follow a man made Gospel or the Gospel of the Lord Jesus Christ (Gal. 1:11,12)?
- If you love as this world loves or as God loves (John 5:42; 1 John 2:15; 4:8,16)?
- If you follow after the spirit of this world or the Spirit of God (1 Cor. 2:4-8; 2:12; 1 John 5:4)?
- If you are a natural man or if you follow after the Spirit of God (1 Cor. 2:14)?

If you would like answers to the above and on issues like AIDS, war, famine, abortion, divorce, homosexuality and the many other issues facing this world today, then we encourage you to turn to the true and living God and His Gospel, as it was preached by Christ and the apostles. "For I certify you that the Gospal which was preached of me is not after man, for I neither received it of man, neither was I taught it, but by the revelation of Jesus Christ" (Gal. 1:11,12).

Please write us if you would like to share in spiritual truth about the true and living God and if you would like to know what it means to REPENT.

(Mailing address removed for this book)

There will be absolutely no soliciting for funds for the gift of LIFE was freely given and freely do we give to all those that believe (Matt. 6:26; 10:8). 51349l26

Advertisement in our paper dated December 26, 1992.

NATURAL	REPENT	SPIRITUAL
BORN IN SIN	Luke 15:10. There is joy in the presence of the angels of God over one sinner that repents.	**BORN OF GOD**
DEATH		LIFE

DOES....

- The Spirit of Christmas have anything to do with the Spirit of God and the birth of the Lord Jesus Christ?

- Good Friday and Easter have anything to do with the death and resurrection of the Lord Jesus Christ?

- The pro life organization, the donation of blood or organs have anything to do with the gift of "Life"?

- Clerical celibacy have anything to do with the service and doctrines of Christ?

- Organized religion have anything to do with Christianity and the teachings of the Lord Jesus Christ?

- Religion have anything to do with "Repentance" to Life and with the transformation and conversion into a child of God?

If you would like answers to the above and on issues like aids, war, famine, abortion, divorce, homosexuality and the many other issues facing this world today, then we encourage you to turn to the true and living God and His Gospel, as it was preached by Christ and the apostles. "For I certify you that the Gospel which was preached of me is not after man, for I neither received of man, neither was I taught it, but by revelation of Jesus Christ" (Gal. 1:11,12),

Please write us if you would like to share in spiritual truth about the true and living God and if you would like to know what it means to REPENT.

(Mailing address removed for this book)

Advertisement in our paper dated December 18, 1993.

NATURAL	REPENT	SPIRITUAL
BORN **IN** **SIN**	Luke 15:10. There is joy in the presence of the angels of God over one sinner that repents.	**BORN** **OF** **GOD**
DEATH		**LIFE**

- Skeletal remains of humans are being discovered that are millions of years old. Therefore, were Adam and Eve the first man and woman who lived appr. 4000 B.C.? Or was Adam the First Son of God (Born of God) who fell to the temptations of this world?

- 6000 years ago the life expectancy for mankind was well under fifty years. Therefore, why did Adam live to be 930 years. (Gen.5:5)?

- When God breathed the breath of life into Adam did that refer to oxygen or God's Spirit?

- What is the tree of life?

- What is the tree of knowledge of good and evil?

- Was the serpent referred to in Gen. 3:1 a snake in a tree or was it the serpent Christ referred to in Matt. 23:33?

- Why was most of the book of Genesis written in parable form (Matt. 13:10-17)?

- Who Is the "Mystery Babylon" referred to in Rev. 17:5?

- How has this whole world been deceived (Rev. 12:9)?

If you would like answers to the above and on issues like aids, war, famine, abortion, divorce, homosexuality and the many other issues facing this world today, then we encourage you to turn to the true and living God and His Gospel, as it was preached by Christ and the apostles. "For I certify you that the Gospel which was preached of me is not after man, for I neither received it of man, neither was I taught it, but by revelation of Jesus Christ" (Gal. 1:11,12).

Please write us if you would like to share in spiritual truth about the true and living God and if you would like to know what it means to REPENT.

(Mailing address removed for this book)

There will be absolutely no soliciting for funds, for the gift of LIFE was freely given and freely do we give to all those that believe (Matt. 6:26; 10:8).   5498579

Advertisement in our paper dated December 11, 1999.

the believers need and look up to their Savior to help them overcome their natural spirit and the spirit of this world, mankind is now judging itself, by claiming to be born again in a natural way. Let me assure them that they will be informed on judgement day that they are dressed with the wrong garment, a garment that they put on themselves but which is not a garment from God (Matt 9:16; 22:9-14; Mark 2:21; Luke 5:36).

I also started to forward correspondence to different church leaders and was even bold enough sometimes to show up on their doorsteps on Sundays during their regular service, only to be shown the highway or have the door closed in front of my face. At one particular Pentecostal institution, they actually chased me down the street when I tried to hand out my testimony to their members. It took quite a while before I learned what was written in the Bible, not to give that which is holy to the dogs or to cast your pearls before swine (Matt 7:6; 2 Peter 2:22).

As we told you earlier, we communicated with several people, like J. Swaggart, the Bakkers and Ralph Rutledge, before God brought them to an open shame. We also communicated with the offices of Billy Graham (see chapter 18), Jerry Falwell, Robert Schuller, David Mainse (100 Huntley Street) and James Robinson, so they would have no excuse when the day comes that they will fall.

We also wrote to then Prime Minister Brian Mulroney of Canada and to Bill Clinton, President of the United States. The time we wrote Bill Clinton was during the time of the "Waco Standoff". We also communicated with Rob Ricks, who was leading the FBI in Waco, and with Dick Deguirin, the attorney for David Koresh.

The views of D. Koresh had nothing to do with God or spirituality as he was leading a small cult just like any other religious denomination.

The reason we wrote to all these people was to show them that this issue had nothing to do with God and that the members of the cult would all destroy themselves. They eventually did. I had even offered my services to communicate with D. Koresh for a peaceful settlement. I know that God would have blessed my work. The only response we received was from the attorney of D. Koresh, thanking us for our message and the earlier warning about his destruction and the destruction of members of his cult.

One of the great manifestations of God is when He moved me to correspond with the then Catholic Archbishop for the diocese of Halifax, Nova Scotia. The main message of my correspondence to him was that God would bring him to an open shame and reveal to the people of Nova Scotia what spirit he and his associates were serving.

The following is a copy of my letter.

April 4, 1988
Mr. James Hayes
Archdiocese of Halifas
P.O. Box 1527
Halifax, NS B3J 2Y3

Dear Sir:
Bad enough that people like yourself do not know what manner of spirit you are of (Luke 9:55 – removed from most translations), but to come out with statements that AIDS is not a punishment of God is so diabolical, that when servants of sin (John 8:34) come out with such statements, it is time to make straight the way of my Lord and Savior Jesus Christ.

Let me first point out that sin is not an act, as this world has made you believe. It is the state you live in, separated from God. Sin is the fruit of the natural man. You yourself were born in sin and under the power of Satan. Yes, you yourself live in sin according to the flesh and the spirit of this world and unless you Repent (change spirits) you will die in your sins (Rom 6:23). You have been deceived as I was for 38 years, when I was a Catholic and walked according to the spirit of this world. And while you think you lead a flock of sheep you are scattering a group of goats in all different directions.

God is the creator of all things. AIDS, cancer and every other disease is a punishment from God as a result of the unbelief of the nations (Ex. 9: 15: 26, Deut 7: 15, 28: 60).

Because you have changed the glory of the incorruptible God into an image made like corruptible man, God has given you up to uncleanness through the lust of your own heart (Rom 1: 23,24). Yes, popes, bishops and priests all walk according to the spirit of this world (Satan) and through philosophy and vain deceit do they spoil man, after their traditions and rudiments of this world, and not after Christ (Col 2:8).

Not only are some of the people, but also some of your popes, bishops and priests of your own institution homosexuals, paedophiles, fornicators and drunkards.

Some even do catch AIDS as a punishment from God, as they live a life separated from God and under the power of Satan (Spirit of darkness, sin). And while they think they know and serve God, they do serve unto them which by nature are not Gods (Gal 4:8). Do you ever wonder why so many of your people are dying in hospitals (stronghold of Satan)? Because you have a form of godliness, but denying the power thereof (2 Tim 3:5).

What right do you have to even make statements on abortion when it is said that Pope Gregory in his time ordered a fish pond in Rome, situated near a convent, drained and at the bottom were found over 6,000 infant skulls. Didn't you know that the province of Quebec records more abortions than any other province while it is predominantly Catholic?

What right do you have to make statements on immortality while the papal household itself has been accused of rape, adultery and all other manner of fornication. I won't even go into detail about some of the other things that have been recorded throughout the history of the Catholic institution.

No wonder my Lord and Savior calls people like yourself hypocrites over and over again. Even names such as fools, blind guides, snakes and vipers were commonly used when Jesus Christ referred to the religious authorities whom eventually silenced Him by hanging Him on a cross.

Unless you Repent (change spirits) you will not understand what I am telling you, for as scripture records: the natural man receiveth not the things of the Spirit of God; for they are foolishness unto him (1 Cor 2:14), and because you are of your father the devil you cannot hear my word (John 8: 43,44), who has deceived all the nations, including yourself (Rev 12:9).

141

Didn't you know that celibacy is a man-made doctrine (Matt 15:9) decreed by Pope Hildebrand Gregory VII in the year 1079 AD? As Paul spoke to Timothy (1 Tim 4: 1-3): Now the Spirit speaketh expressly, that in the latter times (since Christ) some shall depart from the faith, giving heed to seducing spirits, and doctrines of devils; speaking lies in hypocrisy; having their conscience seared with a hot iron; forbidding to marry.

Jesus never imposed such rules, Peter was married and Paul states that bishops were to have one wife and could have children (1 Tim 3: 2,4).

It is for this reason I wrote to you, that your eyes may be opened, that you may turn from darkness to light and from the power of Satan unto God (Acts 26:18), that God peradventure will give you Repentance (changing of spirits) to the acknowledging of the truth; and that you may recover yourself out of the snare of the devil, who is keeping you captive at his will (2 Tim 2: 25,26).

Once God would remove the veil which is upon your heart (2 Cor 3:15) you would no longer deceive the people of this nation. God would also set you free from the Mystery Babylon, the mother of harlots (Catholic institution) (Rev 17:5), through whom all the nations have been made drunk with the wine of her fornication (Rev 17:2). God would also show you that the golden cup you hold in your hands is the filthiest cup of all (Rev 17:4).

And you still wonder why nations are being punished with a disease such as AIDS.

There shall be great tribulation, such as was not since the beginning of the world to this time, no, nor ever shall be (Matt 24:21).

You blind guides, AIDS is only the tip of the iceberg. To fear the Lord is the beginning of wisdom; and the knowledge of the holy is understanding (Prov 9:10).

In the love and service of my Lord and Savior Jesus Christ.

Signed: Andy G. van den Berg

Not long after my correspondence, God uncovered what had been covered and revealed what had been hidden for so long. The following years there were more sex scandals involving priests and religious workers than anyone was able to keep track of. While priests were going to jail, the Archbishop stepped down (or resigned in disgrace, we will never know) not too long after.

To give you, as readers, a better understanding of our work as Soldiers for Christ, I will give you the history of the events of our communication with another Catholic authority, a bishop in Eastern Canada. Perhaps you will come to the knowledge then why our Lord and Savior referred to the religious authorities as snakes and vipers, as many of the accusations he made against us, is what they accused our Lord and Savior of.

This Bishop wrote a weekly column in our local newspaper about so-called religious doctrines. In 1991 we forwarded to him a copy of our testimony along with information on "The Mystery Babylon", the process of Repentance, the history of several religious celebrations, the Shroud of Turin, etc.

The following is a copy of our letter.

November 12, 1988
Mr. Colin Campbell
P. O. Box 1330
Antigonish, NS B2N 2L7

Dear Sir:

Please find enclosed which is self-explanatory to those who believe in Jesus Christ. However, to someone who has been deceived his whole life it is mere foolishness (1 Cor 2:14).

Yes, Satan (spirit of darkness) has deceived this whole world (Rev 12:9) and while you think you know and serve God in truth you are a deceitful worker, transforming yourself into an apostle of Christ (2 Cor 11:13). And no marvel, for Satan himself is transformed into an angel of light (2 Cor 11:14). If it were possible he would deceive even the very elect (Matt 24:24). But thanks be to God who has opened my eyes as I was blind for 38 years and did service unto them which by nature were no Gods (Gal 4:8).

You yourself, were ordained by men (Gal 1:1) and preach according to the wisdom of this world (1 Cor 2:4-8).

I myself was ordained by God (John 15:16) who has taught me in all things (John 14:26).

I do not seek to please men for if I pleased men (as you try in vain), I should not be the servant of Christ. But I certify unto you that the Gospel I preach is not after man. For I neither received it of man, neither was I taught it, but by the revelation of Jesus Christ (Gal 1:10-12).

It is my hope that you will turn to the living God (Repent) so that your eyes may be opened that you will turn from darkness to light and from the power of Satan unto God (Acts 26:18) that you may receive forgiveness of sins and inheritance among them who are sanctified by faith that is in Christ.

I would be pleased to answer any questions you may have that I may help you and show you the ways of my Lord and Savior Jesus Christ and that you may come to know all those that are Christians and those that belong to the true church, the Body of Christ.

In the love and service of my Lord and Savior Jesus Christ.

Signed: Andy G. van den Berg

This is what he wrote in his column a little time later.

Spiritual Arrogance Blinds One To God

How does the expression go? Misery loves company. One of my non-fans, a person working hard for my conversion, tells me I am a deceitful worker who thinks that he knows and serves God. As you might have guessed, this person says that he walked in blindness for 38 years in the Roman Catholic Church.

There is nothing exceptional about this. I have been reading similar claims from people for the last 40 years. The lists of sins, heresies and faults of the church are about the same now as then.

However, the sweep of condemnation and the arrogance of the writer take on a new tone. The message is clear – only he is right and the rest of the Christian churches have led the people into evil and darkness.

Sadly, this sort of material can still confuse people. An amazing number of ordinary Christians cannot detect scissors-and-glue use of the Scriptures. More than once I have run into people who felt oppressed by such leaders. Sometimes, they have had family members who have joined the cult-like churches. The first goal of these people is to show their peers that remaining in the Roman Catholic Church is following the will of the devil.

You had better have many hours if you want to dispute the points raised, one by one. As a tip, I will tell you that the people do not have the great knowledge of the Bible that they may seem to have.

Get them away from snippets that are taken out context and their fortress collapses. Ask them what are the purposes of the chapter, the book and the section of the Bible. When context comes into play, they often begin to look silly.

The fundamental question is to ask about the kind of God that they preach. Behind their scissors-and-glue biblical quotations is a vengeful, hateful, demanding task-maker who, is certainly not God the Father revealed in Jesus.

Challenge them to write a description of their God as taken from their literature. You will find it is not the God of the Gospels and certainly not the God in Jesus. Challenge them on their own turf – the Bible. However, take the Bible in context, rather than snippets.

In one of the mailings, I received copies of letters to Christian leaders. At the end of each was an offer to answer all questions. The implication is obvious – only I can lead you to God. If this is not spiritual arrogance, I don't know what is.

I raise the matter, for some good people have been led into upset, confusion, family discord and hardship by such teaching. We need to instruct our people to see the love and peace that are proclaimed in Jesus.

The Bishop

My words to the Bishop are the same as they were more than 10 years ago.

He doesn't know what spirit he is of and what spirit he serves. Only by turning to the true and living God and through repentance will he ever come to the knowledge of the true and living God and the Lord Jesus Christ.

Only then will he come to know who his real father is today. You may have also noticed that the Bishop is guilty himself of the very things he is accusing us of. They may have studied many years of theology but they have no knowledge of anything in the Bible as they are blinded from the truth. They use little snippets, e.g., God is love, but they could not explain when the Bible speaks of the love of the world and how it is enmity with God and that worldly compassion works death. After his false and public allegations we even gave him an opportunity to put all his so-called knowledge to the test and invited him to a public debate but as expected we never heard back from him.

Two years later, in February 1993, when the scandals about sexual abuse by priests were starting to break, the Bishop wrote a column entitled "Celibacy Truly Gift of God, Blessing In Catholic Church". The only truth in the column was how the doctrine of celibacy entered into the world. You can also find this in the writing on the

Mystery Babylon. But what he wrote about its history did confirm that it is a man-made doctrine. Otherwise most of what he wrote otherwise on the subject was diabolical. At one point, he wrote that the vow of celibacy meant that the person plans to live a life of prayer, a life of union with his peers, and a ministry in which he can form life-giving relationships with others. Otherwise, it is a curse, not a blessing.

The Bible teaches us that they use great swelling words but they have no idea what they are talking about. Well, if the Bishop thought that celibacy was a blessing it certainly looked like a curse to the rest of the world.

In the following years, according to the headlines in the papers, we learned that most of the sex scandals in the province were in his diocese and we even saw a number of his priests serve jail time. At one point the Bishop really put his foot in his mouth when he accused the boys involved in the sex scandals of willful participation, otherwise it would have been impossible, and could possibly not have happened. There was even a general public outrage over these incredible comments.

In 1994 he also wrote a column claiming that an "Infant's Baptism Marks A Person For Life". I wrote the following to the editor of the paper, in response to his column. It was published on July 30, 1994.

> Dear Editor,
> The recent claim by a Catholic Bishop that an infant's baptism marks a person for life is in opposition to everything the Word of God teaches us, as is his claim that the Catholic Institution has been guided by the Holy Spirit throughout its history. Such claims are a natural transformation (2 Cor. 11:13-15).

During the Inquisition, followers of the Roman Catholic Church were directly responsible for the death of millions of people using the most torturous, bizarre and cruel means the church leaders could imagine.

During the last decade, sexual abuse cases involving Catholic Bishops and priests are so widespread that, by one informed estimate, Catholic Institutions have paid out $500 million (this was in 1994) in out of court settlements. Is this a church guided by the Holy Spirit? Is God a liar or did Christ come in vain (1 John 3:8,9)?

In order to be saved, mankind needs to be born again, not of corruptible seed (natural birth) but of incorruptible means and by the Word of God (1 Peter 1:23). This is only made possible through repentance, i.e., to turn from darkness to light and from the power of Satan unto God (Acts 26:18). To teach otherwise is to deceive the people of this world through man-made doctrines (Rev 12:9), which are in opposition to Christ's teachings.

Infant baptism is not a mark for life. It is a mark for eternal death until one becomes born again (I John 3:5-7).

Andy G. van den Berg

During a recent visit with friends in Colorado one of the headlines in their local paper read: Another Catholic diocese faces bankruptcy over sex cases. The article explained how the Catholic Diocese of Tucson would likely become the second American diocese to file Chapter II bankruptcy to avoid potentially crippling judgments in 20 pending sex abuse cases. The move would follow the decision by the Archdiocese of Portland, Oregon, to file for bankruptcy protection in July. It ultimately could lead to the closure of parishes, schools and ministries, as well as claim a cut from the collection plate each week. On December 27, 2004, The USA Today reported that the Boston Archdiocese is shutting down or consolidating 83 churches in response to declining attendance, a shortage of priests and financial pressure caused in part by the clergy sex-abuse scandal.Even common sense would tell anyone, unless one is spiritually blind, that this is certainly not a church guided by the true and living God.

I have a brother-in-law who studied for twelve years in the seminary to be a priest. But, instead of being ordained for the priesthood, he married one of my sisters. Now, he even has a different doctrine from the Bishop's (as if there isn't enough division). My brother-in-law after twelve years of studies informs me that everybody is a child of God. He totally dismisses the claim by the Bishop that a person needs to be baptized. I keep reminding my brother-in-law that if everybody is born as a child of God then there was no need for Jesus Christ to come into this world, for Christ came to destroy the works of the devil. But, like the Bishop, after all the years of studying and learning of the wisdom of this world (theology), he has no knowledge of Satan (the spirit of this world), the devil, the sinful nature of mankind, the Bible, God or Jesus Christ.

For anyone that follows the spirit of this world, the things that I wrote to the Bishop are hard to understand and mere foolishness. Most people, like the Bishop and my brother-in-law, will even think that some of it is evil. But we will remain steadfast in opposition to the spirit of this world and, as the Bible teaches us: they are deceitful workers and blind guides.

Shortly after our last communication with the Bishop, he discontinued his weekly column and eventually retired (or resigned in disgrace, we will never know).

The unfortunate thing is that people will not want to acknowledge that they are deceitful workers and that they are blind guides, for after a while they will just fall into the trap of following after someone else. After Jimmy Swaggart was brought to an open shame on two different occasions there were still many people that continued to attend his services. After all the sex scandals in churches of all different denominations, people still cannot see what spirit they serve. This is why the Bible teaches in John 3:19 that they continue to prefer to follow the spirit of darkness (Satan) rather than the spirit of light (God).

As we go forth with our testimony, we have come to recognize and know that the religious authorities and political leaders will do anything they can to stop us from preaching the message of truth. We also understand the principalities and powers we are confronting in our work and the many obstacles we will face.

They will falsely accuse us, just as the Bishop did in his column, and they will even call us evildoers. As it was in the days of our Lord and Savior Jesus Christ, the religious authorities and political leaders (they serve the same spirit) truly believed that they served the true God, but when He dwelled amongst them, they crucified Him. Times have not changed over the last 2000 years. The situation is the same today as we have learned ourselves during our journey of the last 20 years.

We have experienced how people have falsely accused us in our own community. Our neighbors have even told other people in the community how they would like to see us move. When our daughter was still living at home before she got married, they told her to inform us that we should move from the subdivision. Another neighbor asked me directly one time: Why don't you move from here? For eight years they have tried everything a fiendish mind is able to come up with, in order to make our lives miserable, in the hope that we would move. Some of the things that they have done most people would describe as idiotic and would even say that some of the things they have deliberately orchestrated are abnormal human behavior. They have falsely accused us for things we have never done in order to turn other people against us. Still, there are some who are taken in by them, as the world loves his own (John 15:18-20).

Despite all this, we feel sorry for them for all the lies they have circulated about us. But through it all we know we will be victorious. God will have his revenge some day and when that day comes, it will come swiftly and without warning.

Nevertheless and despite the obstacles before us, we will go forth as the soldiers for Christ. With the wisdom and knowledge of God, we will continue to be encouraged and comforted by the words: greater is He that is in you, than he that is in the world (1 John 4:4).

NATURAL	REPENT		SPIRITUAL
BORN IN SIN			BORN OF GOD
DEATH			LIFE

The Future

Even the devil knows that something is drastically astray. With events that are unfolding today, it is difficult to understand how some people can still think that everything is all right and that world problems are the same today as they have always been. On February 19, 2005, a CNN Internet headline stated that "Catholic Bishops announced that they received 1092 new allegations of sexual abuse against at least 756 Catholic priests and deacons." What is God trying to tell the people of this world? I know by listening to a lot of people, that they are confused and all I can say is that there is no need for anyone to be confused. The message we preach is as clear as looking into a mirror. It is a simple message for anyone that wants to understand the true and living God.

The most important thing to understand is that it is a free gift: you do not have to go anywhere and you can find God in the comfort of your own home. Just go into your room and close the door. The most important words spoken in the Bible for the sake of your conversion are the following:

YOU NEED NOT THAT
ANY MAN TEACH YOU (1 JOHN 2:27)

You don't need hours of instructions from us. This book has explained everything you will ever need to know. The whole purpose of this book is to help you understand the mystery of God and what spirit you are of. You have the Bible as the confirming word for everything you need or want to know, and those words will start to speak to you as God reveals Himself to you. You will also come to know Christ as the living God and, above all, you will come to the knowledge, whatever your walk in life may have been, that you never knew Him and that you were separated from Him. You will also come to know another spirit, a spirit that by nature you were born with. A spirit that controlled your mind in every way and that deceived you into believing that he is a god.

Do not listen to anyone that you hear on television, as it is the greatest tool the devil has today to deceive the nations. Through television the world has changed faster (not for the better) in the last 50 years than in the last 2000. The Bible teaches us that the Spirit of God cannot be received by this present world and the devil would never allow anyone the use of television to spread God's message.

Even the devil knows that, eventually, his time will be up and even some of his servants are preaching the end of times lately. Please do not listen to those deceitful workers, as only the Father knows when Christ will return.

Do not be alarmed over the breakdown of the family and the value system. As the Bible teaches us, don't involve yourself with the affairs of this world. God knows full well what is happening and could change it all with the blinking of an eye. Until that glorious day, remain steadfast in your calling from God.

Besides religion, there are many other forms of bondage. Something that has become very prevalent the last few decades is the ownership of pets. Even the apostle

Paul warned people of the worshipping of four-footed beasts (Rom 1:23). Some animals get more attention today than most kids will ever experience.

I have personally witnessed many people that experience problems in their personal relationships that find it easier to share their affections with dogs, cats and every other animal imaginable, than relate to a spouse, child or another human being.

Before people became so obsessed with animals, people used to take them behind the barn if there was something wrong with them. Today, people will spend thousands of dollars on an operation for their little pooch, even if they can't afford it. Instead, they will let their children go without, so they can have their little animals to care for. I recently heard a report that the pet-food industry alone is a five billion-dollar industry.

Fifty percent of the children in this world today still go without enough food. Please open your eyes. Really, it doesn't take a lot of thinking to find out whose Kingdom this is.

We live in a world of mass confusion. Simplicity has given away to massive selections of everything to add to this confusion. How many religions are there throughout this world? Remember the days when we only had white and brown bread. Today we have whole aisles in stores of every kind of bread you can think of. Or the day when we only had Corn Flakes as a prepared cereal for the breakfast table. Today we have long aisles in the stores lined with everything from large selections of cereals, snacks and soft drinks to all the different kinds of cat and dog food. Has your dog or cat told you recently which brand it prefers?

Another stronghold of Satan and form of bondage where the devil has most people's minds twisted in knots with total confusion, is in the area of their physical afflictions and their dependency on the medical profession. It is certainly the most difficult area to overcome and the devil (natural spirit) will use this area to its full extent. Believe me, we know, most people will not believe our message for this reason alone. Because of years of conditioning they cannot comprehend that there is a God that has power over the flesh (our bodies). Never before in the history of mankind have we seen as many hospitals as today. We have clinics, doctors and specialists for every ailment you can imagine.

Some people will froth at the mouth if you tell them that God will set them free from their doctors and medical profession. For some people I know, it seems that is all they have to live for. Their illnesses, diseases, pains, aches, doctors, specialists, pills and remedies are the only things they can talk about. You would be shocked by the number of operations that are not necessary but are performed each day for the sake of the gain of money alone.

When I first immigrated to Canada and suffered from numerous ailments, I was told that I needed surgery on my neck. I was diagnosed with a so-called compressive lesion between the second and third vertebra. I would have had to go through six months of convalescence and there was even a risk that I could have wound up in a wheelchair.

Thanks be to God, I decided not to proceed with the operation. I also thank God for protecting me even then.

When a person gets to know God, the story of Job becomes very real, as a person will come to know the struggle between Satan and God in his/her own life. In my early years and the above times, Satan would have destroyed me if he could have, but God protected me from his destructive hands.

When I grew up, my mother had only aspirins in the house for a family of nine children. Today, most people take so many pills and other remedies that they need an organizer to know what to take each day. It is quite common for people to take over 10 pills a day for every ailment you can possibly think of. When you walk through drugstores, there are more remedies than body parts these days.

Today you hear about every type of transplant you can imagine. Years ago, people were getting their jaws broken to correct their teeth, then it was knees that they were working on and the last few years everybody needs a new hip or some other joint.

Nevertheless, I have good news to share with all those that believe. When God reveals Himself to you, He will set you free from the medical profession and from every disease you suffer. He already knows where your pain is and what is ailing you. He knew it before you even went to your medical practitioner. Believe me, He does not require you to have an X-ray or a blood test to determine what your medical problem is. He already knew before you were born. He will help you overcome the spirit of this world and He will make you grow in faith, so that you will be able to withstand even the biggest tests, including your physical afflictions.

Please place your trust in God and not the spirit of this world. At the time I am writing this book, we are facing another federal election in Canada and one of the leading issues seems to be health care. Once you know the true and loving God, you will understand how all of the politicians are just grasping for straws. While they make promises with great swelling words, the cost of health care will grow so rapidly that governments will not know where to obtain all of the money required to cover the costs. While they continue to make promises of reduced waiting times for operations and diagnostic procedures, things will only get worse and worse. With all of the media coverage it has become clear that political leaders have set their own personal ambitions for their own gain rather than serving the people of the nation.

While religious leaders have asked for peace for thousands of years and political leaders continue to promise peace that is only overshadowed by mass confusion, things will rapidly worsen as a result of mankind not being willing to adhere to God's teachings and the call for repentance. The most lucrative crimes today are normally initiated by those in high positions of trust, including religious leaders, politicians, senior executives and senior investment brokers.

On June 6, 2004, the world celebrated the 60th Anniversary of the landing on the beaches of Normandy. On that day, I read in our local paper that the fate of today's world hung on the courage, strength and faith of those men bobbing in the choppy English Channel. How wrong they were. The fate of this world (Satan's Kingdom) has already been destined. Every war mankind has ever fought has all been in vain. Your fate has to do with your personal decision and call to repentance. Nothing else should matter to you.

Once again, place your trust in God. It is only through Him that you will be able to overcome the spirit of this world (1 John 5:4,5). Resist the devil and he will eventually flee. God has power over all flesh. He is the potter and you are the clay. He will mold you and refine you like gold tested in fire. Above all, do not fear, for He is with you – but rather fear God, as it is written in the Scriptures in Proverbs 1:7: The fear of the Lord is the beginning of knowledge: but fools despise wisdom and instruction. Or as written in Proverbs 9:10: The fear of the Lord is the beginning of wisdom: and the knowledge of the holy is understanding. Also in Job 28:28 it reads: Behold, the fear of the Lord, that is wisdom; and to depart from evil is understanding.

Our prayer is that God will help you and open your eyes in your search for the truth.

1 JOHN 4:6
HE THAT KNOWETH GOD HEARETH US;
HE THAT IS NOT OF GOD HEARETH US NOT.

Please feel free to contact us
through our Web site:
www.aworlddeceived.ca

The Web site also details
more current and new
revelations since the
publishing of this book.

Notes and References

All content of this book was made possible by inspiration of God.

Job 32:8
But there is a spirit in man: and the inspiration of the Almighty giveth them understanding.

John 6:45
It is written in the prophets and they shall all be taught of God.

John 21:15
For I will give you a mouth and wisdom, which all your adversaries shall not be able to gainsay nor resist.

2 Tim 3:16
All scripture is given by inspiration of God, and is profitable for doctrine, for reproof, for correction, for instruction in righteousness.

1 John 2:27
You need not that any man teach you.

HISTORICAL FACTS - Chapter 7, 10 and 11

Babylon Mystery Religion - Woodrow